THE ART OF INFLUENCING PROJECT SUCCESS

POSITIVELY ACCELERATE PROJECT OUTCOMES
WORKING FROM HOME OR THE OFFICE

NICHOLAS FERGUSON

Difference Press

Washington, DC, USA

Copyright © Nicholas Ferguson, 2020

All rights reserved. No part of this book may be reproduced in any form without permission in writing from the author. Reviewers may quote brief passages in reviews.

Published 2020

DISCLAIMER

No part of this publication may be reproduced or transmitted in any form or by any means, mechanical or electronic, including photocopying or recording, or by any information storage and retrieval system, or transmitted by email without permission in writing from the author.

Neither the author nor the publisher assumes any responsibility for errors, omissions, or contrary interpretations of the subject matter herein. Any perceived slight of any individual or organization is purely unintentional.

Brand and product names are trademarks or registered trademarks of their respective owners.

Cover Design: Jennifer Stimson

Editing: Cory Hott

CONTENTS

1. Projects. People. Paranoia. Possibilities	1
2. My Problems. My People. My Possibilities	11
3. How It Works from 50,000 Feet	23
4. Movement, Force, Momentum, and Project Resistance	29
5. Relating Perspective and Desire to Project Observation	47
6. Awareness of Problems and Possibilities	67
7. Reflecting the Success You Want Forward	87
8. Emotional Indicators of Project Success	111
9. Empowering Your Success or Failure Stories	131
10. Tools and Techniques for Consistent Improvement	145
11. Obstacles and Bumps along the Way	159
12. Relief from Project Stress, Belief in Project Success	167
Acknowledgments	177
About the Author	179
About Difference Press	181
Other Books by Difference Press	183
Thank You	185

To all my friends across space and time, thank you for your relationships, thank you for the expansion, and mostly, thank you for being somewhere I allowed love to happen.

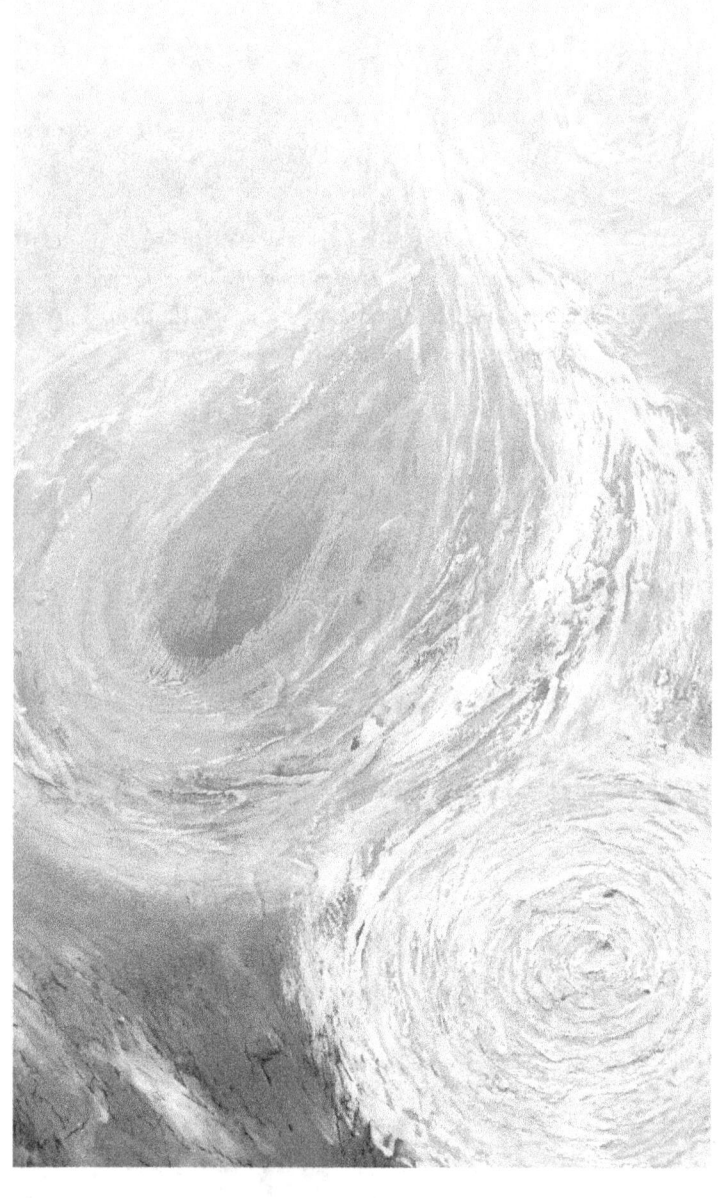

1

PROJECTS. PEOPLE. PARANOIA. POSSIBILITIES

"Leadership is the art of getting someone else to do something you want done because he wants to do it."

— DWIGHT D. EISENHOWER

This quote from Dwight Eisenhower summarizes the best concept in leadership, projects, and team dynamics – simply that others doing something from their desire is most powerful and most beneficial for the leader too.

What I know about you at this point in time is that you are a human being experiencing a life full of expression and perceptions completely unique to you and you alone. I think that's the coolest. Consider this thought for a while with me, and then we'll get back to the book and your project leadership.

You, since being conceived as the result of co-creation, have been creating a life experience that is completely and one-hundred percent unique to you. How incredible is that? Seriously, have you ever looked out into the universe on a dark night and pondered? Have you looked at pictures from the Hubble telescope of galaxies and cosmic formations of billions and billions and billions of stars and realized that your experience is completely unique and so are all the other awarenesses in the universe? It's incredible, and I think it makes you uniquely in control of your life experience whether you understand that right now or not.

In living your life, I know that you've built up awareness of aspects of your life. First, you know yourself to be a physical being on the gorgeous planet Earth, which spins effortlessly, dancing with the other objects in our sun's gravitation. I know that, as a human, you likely rarely think of this effortless ease of the Earth and cosmos and instead focus on the things in your life that have resistance and aren't flowing with effortless ease. I know that these things have a variety of ways you categorize them, and these categories have a variety of emotional identities and attachments with them.

In these categories, I know there are aspects of your business and the thoughts and perceptions you have about your industry, your competitors, the local and global economy, the weather, people on the teams, the vendors you work with, the clients, the flow of money, the prospect of the future, the glory or horror of the early years, and how things changed and what is and isn't working. You have unique perceptions of all of them and so much more, of course. For the sake of needing to focus this book somewhere, this book will be about the perceptions of the projects and people who make up the teams for those projects. I honor and love that you have unique perspectives of your projects and people; I *love* it, and you should too. Remember, you have a unique perspective in this universe, and it means so much that you are focusing it on these projects and people.

As you read this book, I must assume that the focus you have applied to these people and projects isn't completely working the way you desire. That's wonderful; celebrate it, for in learning what you don't want, you are defining more and more of what you do want. Now, you are wondering how to get what you do want when all you currently see is what you don't want. As a hint, it's impossible in a world where seeing is believing; it's always possible in a world where believing is seeing.

PROJECTS. PEOPLE. PARANOIA.

Projects can be so frustrating. You just want them to move faster. You just want them to be finished so you can move onto the next project. You feel something inside that endlessly drives you from a current sense of being incomplete to a measurement of that completion.

You want to know your people and teammates are at least competent, and at the most, are rock stars capable of everything they are responsible for delivering. You want to believe that your projects are meaningful. You want these projects to create change in your satisfaction, your teammate's satisfaction, and your employee's happiness, and you want them to drive more revenue to the business in one aspect or another.

Recently, the 2020 pandemic threw another wrench in the works as most of the world came under new concepts of lockdown. Those fortunate enough to be able to continue through modern technology switched to a forced work-from-home environment. This is the least ideal of all situations for your projects. You have found that being together in an office gives simplified oversight and control over the management of the project. It gives daily comfort to feel projects tangibly – and now this. The team – the company, for that matter – was forced to work from home on short notice. The business doesn't want to change the delivery schedule, even in the new world of work from home and social isolation. How is it possible to get this going?

Before the pandemic and the end of social gatherings, you would see your team at the office each day. You could see what your team members were working on and you could stay on top of those couple of employees who daydreamed, keeping them focused on their work. Now remote, how can you make this happen? How can you stay on top of their work? You just know your employees are slacking off and playing games or watching TV instead of working. You just know it; you tell yourself this as you look for evidence and proof of their progress.

That's when it happens; you remember how it felt when your manager didn't trust you and hounded you for updates, when you didn't quite work up to your current standard of awesome and were still figuring it out. You remember how much pressure you felt and how lousy it was to have him driving you the way he was, but you made it through and came to learn that was best when projects weren't looking so good.

You need to come down on the staff and make sure they know they need to deliver more, they need to work harder, and they need to show evidence of improvement and output. You call a meeting. You tell them that they just aren't producing enough, and that, as a team, you need to output 400 percent from the three people doing the work. You tell them that because you need more insight into what they are doing, you are requiring they use a new project planning tool. You emphasize how this new project planning tool will help keep everybody aligned and on the same page.

After the first week using the new tool, business looks better and you feel some relief, but by the third week, everybody has gone back to their old habits, and they aren't using the tools. Your fears of the project not making delivery come bouncing back like the weight from a crash diet. Not to mention, you are now working from home and can't see your employees' work. You've implemented tools to help see the number of hours people put in, but you feel they are working poorly together in this environment, and you long to get back into the office, in the same space together. You even go so far as to ask the business leaders if you may push the projects back because you don't feel they will make their delivery. The business gives some room for the delivery and adjusts, but not once does this give you a feeling a relief; it's just prolonging the sense that this project can't be completed in time with the available staff, the problems with the remote work environment, and the conditions of the world. You talk more to your manager, and they approve another resource from another part of the company to help. This new resource will eventually be useful, but right now, they are green on the project and must be trained to do some of the work, which, of course, you don't have time for either.

What in the world can you do to help this situation? It seems that all aspects are against you. There is no way to succeed, and you will not deliver that agreed-upon solution in the agreed timeframe. You find yourself so stressed that the interactions with your coworkers and team stop feeling fun and energetic; they feel like a drag and are so much effort. You just want people to understand the importance of these projects and to show their amazing skills. You are even questioning whether you need a new team entirely because you've lost faith in the current one.

This is a brutal place to be. Virtually everything that you do from this position seems to get worse. There are so many reasons to be unhappy with where you are, and they are all true in your perspective; in this world, seeing is believing. There are so many reasons to tell the business that you cannot succeed, and again, this is all true in your perspective of seeing is believing. However, what are the reasons that you can succeed? How are you succeeding even now with this focus on failure? What is working? Surely, something is working out. Still, maybe it is not; maybe it is all crappy, and you are the leader of a crappy team in a crappy world pandemic and feel out of luck on yet another crappy project. This book will help guide you along a path toward understanding how even in crappy circumstances, you can focus on that which feels better and as you do and believe it more and more, what you are seeing in the world will change. Believing is seeing.

POSSIBILITIES.

What can you do? There is so much you can do – so much. I'm not promising that this current project you're working on can turn around and be delivered on time. There is likely so much existing momentum toward its resolution that you aren't in control of it at all, but you can start to improve it. You can improve the next project by preplanning how you want the experience to be, and you can improve your mood about this one right now. Yes, right now – you can do it *right now*.

The only one responsible for the mood is you. I'll teach you how and why in the coming chapters of this book. I'll base this understanding on the laws of the universe as you understand them in the space and time continuum. I'll show you how to consistently power yourself so you are the most advantageous to your team, your staff and coworkers; in fact, everybody who crosses your path will feel the improvement you radiate after you read through and understand the concepts of this book. Will it fix this current project? Yes. Will you deliver it on time? I can't say, as there are too many variables, and I don't know the timeline. I can say that, through understanding the steps and concepts in this book, you will accomplish your goals for this and all projects. You will see how the team is thriving in a work-from-home environment or from the office. More importantly, you will feel relief in your life, and you will feel less stressed. You will feel hopeful and have possibilities that you may not have felt for years. Additionally, you will feel worthy of your success and your team's success.

I understand that the project has constant blockers. It seems that when you overcome one, three more appear. I understand that you have pressure from your management to accomplish the tasks and projects. It seems that everything has been stacked against you, and success is impossible. This is never the case, and I'll teach you how to adjust the perspective so you can focus on the solutions over the problems. Both are valid focus points, but you don't want to have bigger problems, right? Instead, you want to solve them. Let's focus on the solutions. I'll also teach you why this matters and how it matters.

There is another aspect of projects not being completed that leads managers and teammates to want to micromanage the resources. There is a concept that this control will lead to faster delivery. In my experience, it isn't ever the case. On the contrary, it just makes employees and coworkers feel untrusted and like they aren't mature enough to work autonomously. It's a brutal cycle to get into and one that most teams and projects encounter periodically as situations shift.

There is a way to bring consistency to this inconsistent world, and I'm going to share it with you in a few chapters. It's empowering and all about you, and it will take the power out of the external conditions shaping the decisions made based on what you believe is true now and empower your emotional indicators toward the solutions you are looking for consistently.

This chapter started with a quote about leadership because this process is about becoming a leader. Whether you are the defined leader of a project team or a team member of a project, this book is all about you empowering yourself to define your life and stories of success in a way that you want.

I'll share right now that this book isn't about the tools to work remotely. I think countless books have been written on that subject. If you need recommendations on toolsets for remote work, investigate Office 365 from Microsoft. It has everything necessary for everyone, from small teams to massive enterprises. That is the last you'll hear me mention toolsets. This book also isn't about structuring projects and defining structures and workflows. Those all are personal to your unique project and perspective. Instead, I'll help you understand how to evolve them with less effort and more success, but I'll not recommend any defined structure for them. I won't for two reasons. The first is you know what is the right size approach for the current lifecycle of your project and team. I don't, there is too much variation possible. The second reason is there are countless books and blogs written to define and help you implement these structures specifically. I'm not an expert in these regards, but I am an expert in abstraction and connection of thoughts and concepts, which is what I'm going to share with you.

This book is about how you can consistently empower your projects and teams remotely or locally by understanding how much your unique focus matters at this moment and every moment you think about anything related to the projects or teams. It's about understanding how this empowerment will lead to the projects getting completed on time, and the teams producing better than ever before, regardless of team members working locally or across the world.

Yeah, it's going to be magic like that. At least, it's my hope for you that by the end, you too understand how magical that unique point of focus you bring to the universe is for you and everything you have interest in.

This book is about getting you to do things that you want to do because you want to do them and don't feel resistance to them. It's about understanding how this indicator of resistance can guide the projects and interactions to always be empowered. It's about self-leadership influencing perspective, which influences interactions, which influence outcomes. It's about finding yourself worthy. Additionally, it's about clarity in what you want, and it's about energy flow. This book is about you allowing the success into your life that you've already created.

I'm so excited to take this journey with you and to share all this understanding. It's the greatest fun and pleasure I've ever had.

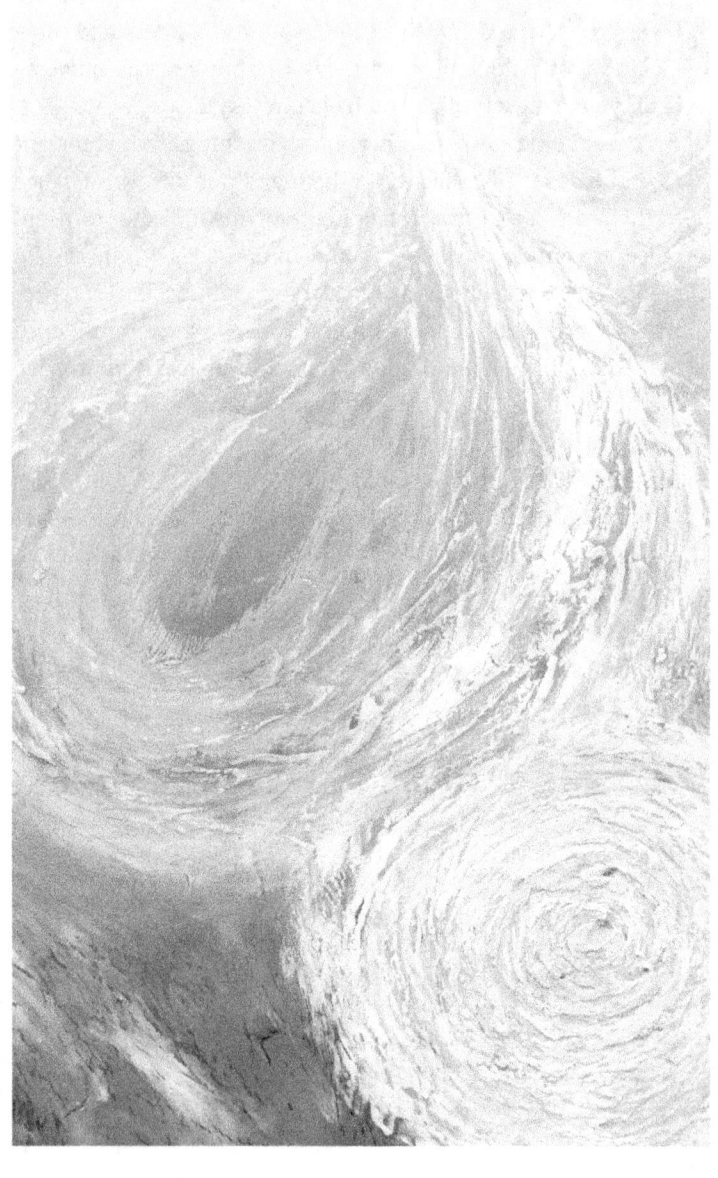

2

MY PROBLEMS. MY PEOPLE. MY POSSIBILITIES

"You never change things by fighting the existing reality. To change something, build a new model that makes the existing model obsolete."

— BUCKMINSTER FULLER

Now, I'd like to share why I'm writing this book. I'm not going to describe why you should listen to me, as that goes against the very nature of why I wrote this book about the concept of self-leadership, which I touched on in the previous chapter. I don't want you to listen to me; I don't believe that it's best for you to take the guidance and direction from somebody else without cause, without reason, and without resonance within you for the message they're sharing. This book has been the culminated manifestation of my life. I've followed a path that was right for me and quite different than the rest of the world, and for that, I often feel joy and peace, and my well-being improves.

I grew up in the Colorado mountains to a typical family – on the outside – with a father, mother, sister, dogs, and cats.

My family experienced its share of abuse, neglect, and struggle, as have most in this modern world. I never cared for school; I struggled to read and found homework to be the worst. The amount of zeroes I had in high school for not doing work was staggering. I failed out of college rapidly and then worked in restaurants and bars for years. I dug the lifestyle, as it was laid back and relaxed. If I didn't like a restaurant, I would get a job at another. It was a great time of life. I experienced what it was to be on my own in some sense. I made money, hung out with friends, and enjoyed it all, but never felt like I was making use of all the talents and abilities I knew I had somewhere in me.

This sounds like somebody you should listen to regarding how to improve project and team performance, right? I know; I wouldn't listen to me at this point, but stay with me a bit longer, it's worth the ride.

MY PEOPLE. MY PROBLEMS.

In my mid-twenties, my mom became quite ill, and I felt a need to make more money to help. Through a series of lucky coincidences, I got hired by Compaq Computer Corporation and was put through a six-week intensive training period to learn how to support their enterprise product line of servers and storage. I continued this work for about a decade and moved up to other positions. I loved it – every aspect. I love technology, and I love learning and growing. I loved the trust and belief that my managers had in me and my dedication to the company, the teams, and the customer's success. I loved being productive. I loved having a job that felt more worthwhile than I did working in restaurants and bars. I loved how good I was at understanding abstract system design, and I loved the people I worked with and the building I worked in at the time.

My mom's sickness didn't improve much. Compaq was bought by HP and pay freezes were created. I needed more money but couldn't find it through HP. I put my resume online and a consulting company in Bermuda offered me a job. I took it for the money, and I wanted to run away from the living situation I was in as well. It felt like my chance to escape and see the world. It was scary to leave everything I knew in Colorado and the safety of my awesome job with HP, but it felt like it was the right choice. Within the first few weeks in Bermuda, I was contracted to work for a hedge fund building out their first datacenter. I've been working for that hedge fund ever since in various roles and capacities.

I've learned so much from the organization. I feel so lucky to have worked with a firm whose entire concept of business is built on integrity and partnership. It changed my perceptions of what powerful people could be like. While I was in Bermuda, I fell in love, got married, and had my son. We later moved back to the United States to help open an office and to experience another aspect of life. While in the U.S., my wife began to dissociate and have some mental health challenges that eventually spiraled out of control. Upon coming home from a business trip, I found a "Dear John" note taped to my garage door and most of my house empty; the most important part of my life, my best friends – my wife and child – were gone. The note effectively said, "I'm out of this and will be in contact when it's right for me. Peace."

My heart literally felt broken. I felt agony and so much physical pain from this sudden loss and the complete shift of all I thought was my life. It was unreal, yet sadly, completely real. Many events transpired, and eventually my son was back with me; courts ruled against her ability to parent, and I became a full-time parent of a two-year-old and a full-time employee trying to grow and maintain a dynamic technology team spread across three countries. For the next couple of years, I sank myself into therapy, parenting, and work, in no specific order. I started taking prescription methamphetamine so I could keep up with the pace and demands of my life to be awake and productive all the time. I started my day at 3:00 a.m. and ended it near midnight every day for a couple of years. On top of the methamphetamine, I would also drink lots of energy drinks, cups of coffee, or any other stimulant to help me keep up with the pace. I was productive; I was a great parent. I was killing myself; I felt hollow.

Eventually, this way of living caught up with me. Eventually, I reached burnout. It was a clear burnout – overwhelming and crippling. I wrote to the founders that I needed time off and I took it. I was depressed at this point and just wanted to sleep, so for the first couple of days, I slept, slept, and slept some more. I stopped taking the pills and didn't need to work twenty hours a day. Slowly, over the month I had off, I started to feel again.

What I know now is that the experience killed my emotions; that was the hollow feeling. From the time my son's mother left, I threw myself into work, various therapies, single parenting, and learned all new technologies possible, just so I didn't or wouldn't feel. That was the biggest problem with my twenty-hour day work lifestyle – it numbed my emotions. Well, it didn't numb my emotions; I numbed them by choice and continued doing it. I shut my emotions down and became completely desensitized to them. I thought the emotions were my weakness and they didn't matter. I thought business needed to be objective and without emotions. I expected my team to work as hard as I did, impossibly and unhealthily hard. I expected them to be as emotionless as I was until I started to feel again. Then, I realized the error in my ways.

As I started to feel again, I also listened to a couple of YouTube feeds and audiobooks. I reacquainted myself with

Abraham-Hicks and started meditating every morning. Within a fairly short time, I started to experience changes in my life. I noticed the days weren't filled with struggle. I noticed that I smiled most of the time. I noticed that I didn't get upset with my son. I noticed a general feeling of positive expectation about what was coming in life. I noticed that there were so many other things I could think about besides how to program or architect another technical solution. I realized that I was in control of my emotional state and the thoughts that went through my head.

As time progressed and I found more and more peace, I went back to work and readjusted my role. I went back and asked to be more of an advisor and mentor than the technical owner of the keys to the castle. There had been enough change from my abrupt time off that it wasn't a big deal for this change to happen, so I met with my team and started to try to convey this new awareness. I so wanted to correct the culture of working oneself to death and emotionless environments. I'd realized that my emotions were an indicator of the power of my alignment with all that I wanted. I realized that emotions needed to be involved in business choices and decisions. I understood that if people could feel and understand their emotions as I had grown to, the power the team could produce was unstoppable. I wanted to find a way to help explain this further.

During a leadership meeting, one of the firm's founders asked a group of the future leaders of the company how to teach intuition to others, how we could power our workforce even more, and then jokingly, if anybody could explain why millennials were so different and challenging. I wasn't quite ready to share all this detail, but I thought to myself, "You know, I can do all those things," so I set out to understand it well enough to be able to share with the company how it worked.

Before I burned out, I helped build a dynamic and amazingly productive team spanning three offices in three countries. I had many growth moments as I tried to manage teams, people, and projects. I had even more growth moments as I learned to hand over duties and responsibilities broadly. I learned how much my belief in the capabilities and overall persona of another person was in my perspective. I learned what worked well and what didn't work well over fifteen years in a highly dynamic environment.

POSSIBILITIES

As I started this chapter off, I learned that the process of this growth and understanding didn't come from seeking it and reading countless books about what others believe is the psychology and philosophy on success and growth. The reason I hated school so much was because I didn't want the world to tell me how it should be seen; I wanted to define and understand why things were the way they were from my knowledge stemming from my understanding. This is the same way I took on technical work; I didn't learn it from books, but from doing and making mistakes and growing in the process. I realized this is the same thing I had been doing with my understanding of life. I wanted to create and define what it meant to me and to understand in my perspective how people and the universe worked.

Over the next year, I continued to meditate daily and continued to be less and less resistant to the changes that came up in life. I started experiencing amazing coincidences. After about a year of meditating daily, I came to a thought – the thought that led to this work that I share here – and that thought led to everything else.

During the summer of 2019, I went on the Abraham-Hicks Alaskan cruise with my son. It was the best time, and the relaxation and well-being I felt was indescribable. During the last of the Abraham seminars, I was called to the hot seat. I asked an obtuse question specifically about my understanding of the universe at that time, and I knew that, before I sat in the hot seat, it was either going to resonate with my understanding or it was going to clarify where I was wrong. The message from Abraham solidified the rest of this work. I didn't realize it at the time, as all I knew then was that I could represent our nonphysical aspect in the same way Einstein represented our physical aspect as a relationship in co-creation through the Theory of Relativity and the equation $E=M*C^2$.

Once I got back home from the cruise and relaxed, my head filled with images and movies of things I didn't understand. I turned on the voice recorder on my phone and closed my eyes and meditated a bit. During that meditation, I felt the desire to speak and talked to my recorder for about forty-five minutes straight. I shared my understanding of the universe and how it all works. It was so clear. I felt goosebumps – thrill bumps – running over my body throughout the session. At this point, it is still the most incredible experience. I then finished the thought flow and came out of the meditation. I was so excited to listen back to what I said, but the recording didn't work. I had five seconds of the whole session recorded.

After that, I was bummed and didn't think I would ever experience that again. I tried to find the thoughts, and I tried to get back to the translation that I'd found, but I couldn't. This might be the first time you've encountered somebody referring to thoughts as a translation. I'll explain in the coming chapters how your awareness creates energetic expansions of awareness in your mind, and these expansions are translated by you through your unique perspective so that you can understand the relationships with your experiences in this time and space reality. For me, at this time, the more I looked for it and tried to get my thoughts to it, the more I grew sad and frustrated that I couldn't get there.

It was at this point that everything made sense to me. I realized how to be receptive to the information flow and how to allow it. I couldn't go looking for it; I had to allow it to come to me. It came to me the first time when I relaxed into being, when I let go of stress, but my focus didn't feel great. In response, I relaxed more and found some happy thoughts. As soon as I found my relaxed state again, the thoughts started flowing to me again. Over the next few months, this became a fun game for me. It seemed that whenever I released my thoughts, I would naturally go back to this intense path of understanding and flow. As I allowed it to come to me more, I was inspired to look up the definition of a word or a concept, and as I did, more of this made sense to me. Effectively, the more I relaxed and felt joy and happiness, the more of this profound understanding would come to me.

I wanted to share it with the world. I wrote it all down; I recorded it, and I talked it through with a couple of friends. I even called my mom and told her I understood the secret of the life and the universe. I think most people thought I was out of it. As I understood more and more, I wanted to share it with the firm I'd worked at for so long. I saw and understood the power that could come from this understanding and way of being. I offered to share it with the founders. I believe my email to them said something as crazy as, "I understand the laws of the universe uniquely now and would love to share what it means with you and hopefully be able to share it with those in the company also interested in deliberate creation." It was so funny, brash, and unexpected coming from a person who had been basically unseen for a couple of years, happily working in the background.

I wasn't sure what was going to happen, but I felt that

was the right path. Well, timing wasn't ideal for them, and they asked me to write a short summary about what I wanted to share, and then we would find a time to discuss it. Well, I wrote three or four different short summaries that were all twenty to forty pages in length. I literally couldn't make this understanding take up fewer pages because I needed to give the basis of what people think now and why it has been misled without fully understanding the entire picture of our experience. Again, it was unexpected coming from me. Still, after writing that a few times and never wanting to share it with them because of the length, I figured I should just write a book about what I now understand. When I came upon The Author Incubator, I knew the program was just right for what I wanted, and I signed up. This book is the result.

Why do you want to listen to me? Well, I'm uneducated by the traditional school systems. I've never been subjected to religious doctrine or perspective at great depths. The understanding I have come to in this book has come from my logical bridging of symbolic concepts and thoughts. I think it's the most brilliant bridging of these concepts that has ever come from humanity, but I'm obviously biased.

When I was a young child, I thought that every point of the universe was conscious. I could see trillions and trillions of dots that looked like pixels everywhere I looked. When I was younger, these dots were the energy of the universe that I was seeing and translating. I also had a rich dialogue with my inner being, the nonphysical aspect of ourselves. I knew the guidance of that voice so well. I remember telling my mom about it when I was in grade school, and she told me I shouldn't tell people that because they would think I was crazy, so it started a path of denying my inner power and worthiness, which built up into the story I shared above.

What I know now for certain is that emotions are so important to us collectively. You shouldn't try to remove them from business. You say things are not personal and try to keep emotion out, but what I'm certain of now is that you should understand the guidance emotions provide you in business or any other aspect of life.

THE START OF AN UNDERSTANDING

This understanding came to me from the processes I will describe in Chapters 4 through 10. I stopped my resistant thoughts and allowed my conscious vibration to rise. As it rose and wasn't contradicted by doubt, these thoughts and translations came to me as occurrences – new thoughts. The moment of occurrence is always a good-feeling thought that you haven't had before. This is what I'll describe later as the new energy coming into your experience. It comes as an occurrence, a new thought, a new emotion, or a new perspective you've not had previously, and they are the thrill of life when you understand what's occurring.

What occurred to me that led to this thought path? It was that the word "human being" could be broken down like this:

Hum an being
Hue an being

Notice that if you rotate the "M" sideways, it becomes an "E." I thought that humans experience this work as vibration and as light, so these two breakdowns made total sense to me. I understood as vibration you "hum," and as light, you are a gradient of a whole at any one time. I understood the "M" and the "E" as a way of displaying the pivot – the valve that humans have of the capability of being. It was from this that I started to look and understand Einstein's equation, for in his equation, the understanding that energy and mass are different manifestations of the same thing started me thinking.

Eventually, I put all the pieces together and formed my theory of reflectivity, which is ultimately shared with you briefly in Chapter 8. The concept is truly simple in all this. The less resistance you have, the faster you move physically and the less time you experience. The less resistance you have, the more powerful your thoughts are non-physically and the less expansion you feel toward them. You are both aspects at the same time; you are being one or the other. You are a human being who is constantly interchangeable and interchanging between physical and nonphysical thought.

Why should you listen to me? Well, again, you shouldn't. You should listen to your own resonance. If what I share resonates with you, then you should investigate its concepts more. If it doesn't resonate with you, move along – nothing to see here.

All of the things I am going to share in this book have come from the simple concept that releasing resistance to thought and movement allows your vibration to naturally rise, and from this higher vibration, your perceptions and thoughts are improved and become more powerful. The less resistance, the more clarity in the translation of the vibration. This book is the summary of what I understand to be the process and why it works based on how you understand the physical world. You are both physical and nonphysical, and you are astounding. I am so excited to share this understanding with you. I'm sure it will resonate truthfully within you too.

I want to share another aspect. I was a technical architect for decades and, six years before the pandemic, built the infrastructure of the firm that allowed full work-from-home capabilities for everybody in the firm. It wasn't truly used until mid-March 2020, when global recommendations to work from home started happening. What this means is that I'm fully capable of writing a book on how to design systems and environments to support amazing work-from-home scenarios. However, what I know is that you can have the best tools and processes available, but if the mental state isn't right for taking advantage of working remotely, you will ultimately be your own failure point. This book is about finding the mental state and empowering yourself and your teams in any scenario that comes up. The success of the work-from-home worker is less about the toolsets and more about the awareness of resistance than anything else. Don't create the mistake of creating more resistance just by being in a remote scenario.

I'll close out this chapter with a brief summary of the points. My life has been full of contrasts that have allowed me to see with clarity the bridging between our physical experience as mass and our nonphysical experience as thought and awareness. I've realized more and more how to explain this bridge's functionality with increasing simplicity and consistency from what has come before. I'm incredibly eager to share this understanding, for there are endless empowering perspectives and possibilities that come with it. I'm excited for you to also begin feeling relief to self-created resistance.

3

HOW IT WORKS FROM 50,000 FEET

"The world as we have created it is a process of our thinking. It cannot be changed without changing our thinking."

— ALBERT EINSTEIN

In the following pages, I'll share with you a new way of perceiving yourself and your reality. It will be a new way of leadership, either self-leadership or in a group setting. I'll share the logic that brought me to this understanding and the laws of nature that you have been using to describe it for over a hundred years – without ever bridging the thoughts of physics and consciousness until now. Well, perhaps they have been bridged many times before – I'm sure they have been – but they haven't been in the clean and concise way I'll share with you.

What's going to come from this understanding is a new way of perceiving the slowness or challenges with projects and the different relationships you have with people.

In Chapter 4, I will discuss Sir Isaac Newton's laws of motion that were written way back in the 1600s, discussing the three laws of motion and the understanding that comes from them, including inertia, momentum, and force. This is pertinent, as I discuss and explain how you can deliberately create your experience and therefore how you are in control of speeding up the delivery of your teams and projects in the office and remotely.

In Chapter 5, I will extend this understanding of motion to the relationships between all objects in motion and how these motions influence project outcomes. I will discuss how it's your relationship with everything that determines your experience. I will discuss time dilation, length warping, gravity lensing, gravity well, kinetic energy, potential energy, and of course, the mass-energy equivalency. I will discuss how it's your observation of these things that is unique to you in the universe and how your relationship with your projects, people, and resources are the results of the influences. I'll discuss what mass is defined by and what it means to you in context of projects success. You will understand how resistance is relative and how decreasing resistance is the key to speeding up everything else. You will learn about co-creation and understand how co-creation has left you with space-time and subjective and objective realities.

In Chapter 6, I will discuss conscious awareness, such as the awareness of the relationship from the previous chapter, the relationship with the motion of a person or an aspect of your project, and observation of it and your subjective translation of it. I'll share the concept that awareness is a nonphysical trait within you, and as such, has unique behaviors but responds to the laws of motion and your understanding of relationships through relativity, just like your physical world does. You will understand that your thoughts and your awareness of them are unique to you. It's your perceptions in this awareness that creates the resistance that is relative to the other aspects of motion. You will start to understand how your awareness creates the resistance to the success of the team and projects.

In Chapter 7, I will extend this concept of nonphysical awareness further by explaining what I call the theory of reflectivity. In this theory, I'll explain how the nonphysical and physical environments are inverses of each other but always respond to the laws of the universe consistently once understood how the two environments differ. I will talk through how this nonphysical and physical awareness manifests in your experience as you think and feel uniquely about those concepts you're developing your relationships with. I will also talk through how these concepts explain your thought process cleanly and are expressed through the individual and their unique perceptions of this universe. You will learn that the reflected co-created environments are the collective and vibrational realities, and these co-create the vibration-expansion continuum.

In Chapter 8, I will talk about how emotions indicate the energy flow through their two aspects, the physical and nonphysical, and you will understand how and why this works. I will discuss the emotional guidance scale and what energy flow means. Additionally, you will investigate the concepts of realization and actualization. I will lightly discuss the Hawkins scale of consciousness and the Abraham-Hicks emotional guidance scale. In all these aspects, you will understand how your emotions change based on your thoughts and your focus. It is this subtle change that guides you to what you want and what you don't want. It's subtle at first and grows in power and momentum over time.

In Chapter 9, you will understand how these concepts lead to your current reality and how the narratives that you chronically tell others and yourself are an indicator of your resistance to this energy flow. You will understand that, as you restrict the flow of energy and growth used to not feel your best, you adapt, and it becomes normal to you. This happens for a variety of reasons; one reason is that you stop feeling your desires happen, so you stop wanting to change and just accept where you are because you grow accustomed to it. For example, you accept the limitations that you knew about yesterday as the limitations you have today. You accept that people on your project team performed a certain way yesterday and will continue to do so today too. While likely feeling lousy about these limitations, your continued acceptance of them day in and day out leaves you desensitized to the lack of energy flow and this lousy feeling. You accept it as-is and just complain about it through the narratives you tell about it. You will learn how it's possible to improve this narrative with consistent ease from wherever you are.

In Chapter 10, you will learn some techniques on how to overcome the resistance that slows down your project and people. You will build upon the understanding from previous chapters that it's resistance that slows you down the most, and you will learn how to be aware of this resistance more and more. You will learn about meditation and how a quiet mind naturally returns to a high energy flow. You will understand why morning momentum can be the most powerful force in your day – if you use it to your advantage. You will understand how increasing your output and results in the world is more about allowing the energy than forcing it. And you will learn why journaling and writing lists of appreciation help increase the speed of manifestation.

Chapters 11 and 12 will be the conclusion of the book. I'll summarize what you learned, and I'll share some obstacles that came up for me and a few others when they first started to change their perceptions to a more powerful position. I'll share why I wanted to share this and how much I want you to understand that the power of changing your project and people delivery speed isn't nearly as much about the force you apply to make things happen as it is about the energy you flow to allow it to happen. I'll offer some more closing advice and ways of contacting me, should you want to learn more or be coached through how to allow more in your life.

EVIDENCE AND PROOF

This is not the typical business book or project book that will walk you through the nuances of blockage and overcoming them in a project manner. Instead, it's about universal law and how you can leverage it consistently in your life. This book specifically applies the concepts to projects and people in new work-from-home environments, but the concepts are applicable to all other situations. It's about focus, energy flow, and how much of it you allow at any moment. As you'll understand by the end of the book, this is about you living the life you created for yourself and embracing the deliberate power to create through your focus.

I'm not going to back up what I'm sharing with loads of scientific works in hoping you find more resonance and belief in the words. I could write a hundred books on various topics sharing the secrets of the universe with you. I could back up everything I say with tons of scientific studies mentioning the concepts I'm describing, but if you can't translate them to something meaningful in your life and define a personal relationship with the understanding, it will never mean anything to you. In other words, I can't possibly write enough to convey a lesson to you that must be learned through your experience, nor can providing scientific-based evidence lead you to understand any better. I'm going to explain from the basis of our understanding of this universe, bridging psychological, philosophical, and even some religious qualities into a more coherent model of our experience. The beauty of this model is that it's consistent across your experiences and always reliant on your mood with your emotions as the basis of the guidance. I will specifically avoid using terminology that has conflicting momentums associated with it. The concepts like God, Mind, Spirit, Soul, Source, Ego, Sub-Conscious mind, Id, Conscious mind, and many quantum terms are avoided throughout the book for the variety of meaning that is already established on the words. I'll take more generalized concepts and bridge them together in a meaningful way.

Remember in the last chapter how excited I got about you as the focus of a unique aspect in this universe? Well, doesn't it make a little sense that the mood you have and the emotions you presently have meant something about the focus – this unique focus – that only you have in this entire universe? Maybe.

I'm so excited to help you get past those blocks that keep you and your projects from flourishing. Let's learn to thrive, and let's learn to leverage the powers of the universe to feel better, deliver more, and empower those who cross your path.

It's easy – really, easy. It's almost insultingly simple once explained, and it's simplistically beautiful. It couldn't be made simpler, which is how I knew the rightness of the design as I understood it. Are you ready?

4

MOVEMENT, FORCE, MOMENTUM, AND PROJECT RESISTANCE

"Nothing happens until something moves."

— ALBERT EINSTEIN

I believe there is a system behind our experience in this space and time continuum. I believe you can leverage this system as you understand the laws inherent within it. Humanity's longest-standing understanding of the laws of motion was initially brought to us in 1657 by Sir Isaac Newton. He gave three rules that much of the modern world has used to comprehend motion for centuries. As you understand these laws better, you begin to understand how they can impact the speed of your projects and people in your world abstractly. As you progress through this book, you'll add more solidity to the abstractness of this thought, making it more concrete for you.

The following is a quick summary of the laws of motion as defined by Newton. The purpose of this book is not to go into depth on any of the scientific concepts discussed since there are countless books that do just that. My purpose is to explain the essence so that I can bridge the concepts of your present thoughts with your relationships to your project and team success.

Newton's first law established what a base frame of reference is; he termed it an inertial frame of reference. An inertial frame of reference is used with classical physics and special relativity to describe a body that is not accelerating, has zero force acting on it, or is at a constant rate of acceleration. He stated in this first law that an object is either at rest, or not moving, and if it is moving, it will continue to move in a straight line at a constant velocity. Velocity is defined as something's speed in a specific direction. This inertial frame established a basis to understand another concept – force – qualitatively. Force itself is defined as strength or energy as an attribute of physical action or movement.

Newton's second law offered a method of quantifying the force described in the first law. The second law introduces the equation of force. Force equals the product of mass and acceleration (force equals mass multiplied by acceleration). It also introduced the concept of momentum, which is defined as the quantity of motion of a moving body as a product of its mass and velocity (momentum equals mass multiplied by velocity). The equation of force also introduced two other concepts – mass and acceleration. Mass is defined as an object's resistance to change in motion, while acceleration is defined as the change in motion over a specific amount of time, so Newton's second law defines the characteristics of how objects move.

Finally, with his third law of motion, Newton described how a single isolated force doesn't exist and that each action has an opposite reaction.

That might be the most simplistic definition of Newton's

laws ever, and I accept that as a good enough basis to discuss applying this understanding as leverage when influencing project and team success.

MAKE IT GO FASTER

"The questions that our society must ask revolve around whether the time-consuming demands of the deep-reading processes will be lost in a culture whose principal mediums advantage speed, multitasking, and processing the next and the next piece of information."

— MARYANNE WOLF

How do these laws impact your projects and people's performance and speed? The knee-jerk reaction you may have is that projects aren't mass in this regard and don't apply to these rules. People are a type of mass, but they don't apply because they have conscious awareness and are autonomous. I'll eventually explain how these apply in-depth. For now, I want to share more of the concepts of these laws.

Newton's first law created an imaginary state known as the inertial frame of reference. In project land, this might be referred to as a "greenfield project," meaning that there isn't movement and mass already assigned to the project. There aren't people already working through it; it's a blank slate, a green field to build from.

This inertial frame of reference works with your understanding of the people and resources related to your project too. You either have history with the people and they are already in motion, or they are in an inertial frame of reference and untested, unproven, and undefined from your perspective.

Your inertial frame of reference for your projects and people comes down to where your thoughts are right now regarding them. Do you have history with the project or is it all brand-new with zero movement from your perspective?

As you come to define what these inertial frames of reference are for your projects and people, you establish what forces will be acting upon them. From the first law of motion, you know that the projects and people will continue to move in a straight line of progress if there aren't external forces in action once they start moving and that external forces will slow this movement down or cause it to change course.

Outside your inertial frame of reference, the forces acting upon a project and people rapidly manifest. People have various experiences in life; they come from various backgrounds, and all have a variety of things occurring in their lives that impact the forces influencing their motion constantly. You all do, and they all impact performances.

The second law from Newton describes that the total force is equal to the product of acceleration and the mass of an object. It also describes momentum, which is defined as the product of its mass and velocity. Momentum is the fairest force in the universe; it just adds more to what is already happening.

Typically, this is the law that matters to you when you want to get your projects and people moving faster; that is, when you want them accelerating. Remember, acceleration is change in velocity over a unit of time. This is the law that helps you understand the interactions that come from that acceleration or what will cause it to slow down. Effectively, the more mass a project has, the more force is necessary to accelerate it; or, in an equation, force is the product of mass and acceleration (force equals mass multiplied by acceleration). In your space-time reality, which is the name sciences gives to what you consider real life, as you will learn in the next chapter, when any mass accelerates, its kinetic energy is increased; as this energy increases, so does its mass increase. Therefore, so must your force increase to maintain acceleration.

What does this mean? Imagine your project as a generic lump of mass. As you start to increase the speed of that project's deliveries, the mass increases; you see this in the scope of the delivery with increases in requirements, technical dept, training, support challenges, vendor involvement, customer and client expectations, and worst of all, the push back from your doubt as these challenges begin to amass and the project begins to slow down.

As you accelerate your people, you tend to notice the more force you apply, the less output you get for the amount of energy you feel you are spending. This is because acceleration also increases mass and drag. You tend to create drag by resisting changes, bickering over choices, pointing fingers of blame, and anything else you can find that allows you to resist.

You can imagine how you create a whole chunk of additional drag with the concepts around working remotely. Depending on you, most, if not all, of the disempowering concepts and stories you come up with are forms of drag and resistance to your projects and people. When you ease the stories you tell, your focus on these points of drag releases resistance. The longer you can maintain this less resistant state by not focusing on the drag, the more momentum builds toward a positive direction. As this momentum builds, it will become the dominant perspective, and you will notice a feeling of relief to this resistance and drag.

As a leader on a team, when these instances occur, you tend to create more force and push harder. As a manager, you might start micromanaging the team because you believe that employees aren't working hard enough, are joking around too much, and need to be more serious. You start to focus on the delivery time window over the actual delivery. There are countless ways that you can create more drag, but the important thing to understand is that, as you increase speed and as you accelerate, you increase the force needed to be applied to consistently keep that accelerated speed.

MOMENTUM

> *"Success comes from taking the initiative and following up...persisting...eloquently expressing the depth of your love. What simple action could you take today to produce a new momentum toward success in your life?"*
>
> — TONY ROBBINS

Momentum is the greatest gift; it is the great equalizer, for everything gains momentum. I love to think of momentum in a business world of projects and people as a train. Trains have one too many engines, one too many cars being pulled by the engines, and they have tracks to follow. The tracks are your road maps, project plans, and staff and personal development plans. Most have been in the process of being built and connected for years. They are, in theory, the paths you will apply force down to move your train. They are smooth and allow less resistance to the motion of the train. They ensure that you are on a path and the path is a stable base to move your project and people through. As the train moves down the track, it gains momentum – the more cars, the more mass, and the more momentum.

Momentum is such a gift when you learn to use it

correctly, but it is a complete nightmare when it gets away from you.

Imagine that train needs to stop or change to another track. Stopping is worst; it requires so much force to stop the train moving because of its momentum and then even more momentum to start moving again. Have you ever watched a long train start moving from a stop? It takes a series of rocking motions to get the train moving forward again and so, so, so much effort. You experience this in projects as you block or stop them. People involved in projects need to be rocked back to movement again; there is always a process to it. Trains stop by applying brakes miles and miles in advance and decelerating. Projects are often stopped or paused because of world and environment changes. The momentum of the stopping is often destructive, creating more drag to overcome in the new directions. Effectively, the contents of the train are protected as the train brakes and slows. It's unlikely that the contents of the project – the people – are likewise protected because, historically, they are not thought of in this way.

It is this people-based momentum that begins to slow things down as it increases. Remember, momentum is fair – super fair – and always creates more where focus is applied. It seems people, while capable of moving past these things, generally hold onto changes like this and build up a grudge in future changes. This grudge or resistance is momentum, but it's not accelerating momentum; it is decelerating momentum. In these instances, you build momentum in an opposite direction, effectively creating even more drag for the next project or the direction change of this one.

The third of Newton's laws of motion states that for every action, there is an equal and opposite reaction. In some sense, that is what I am describing in the preceding paragraph. Newton uses this law to explain how there is not an isolated movement in the universe and that all movements have a balance with another movement. I was describing how a changed or canceled project can, and will, impact the momentum of the people working on that project. This is effectively the opposite reaction to the slowing or canceling of the project.

The interesting aspect of this interaction is that, without conscious, deliberate attention, any change in direction leads to a significant amount of drag being created, and that drag, of course, creates a need for more force to be applied or it will decelerate. I'll explain further.

For example, project A was going forward well enough. There were some challenges with it; one of the team members wasn't holding his weight in the view of the rest of the team, there were some directional squabbles, the business questioned the need for the project, and the project team started to doubt the value and their ability to complete it on time. This is full of drag and resistance to moving forward. I'd say it's doomed and won't be completed in this format. Even if it is completed, it's highly unlikely the results will be the desired results in the business perspective.

As the project needs to accelerate, more pressure is applied to the team members. They are asked to work nights and/or weekends; they are asked to cut some corners that don't seem to matter as much; and they are told that if they don't accomplish this, they won't be rewarded, and they might not have a job, or any number of random threats companies like to offer.

The number of projects I have encountered in this scenario is significant. Most seem to have this as a basis at some point in the project lifecycle. Applying what you know about the laws of motion now, with the current momentum, the project is doomed; it's obvious. However, because you know that each action has an equal and opposite reaction, you can work with it. The natural path for most humans is to apply more pressure to the team, telling them to do more. They need to apply more force effectively and produce more so that the project can accelerate (force equals mass multiplied by acceleration). This application of force without decreasing the drag or resistance will slow the project down, as you will learn in the next chapter because the increased speed increases the mass of the project and the force necessary to move it.

From this place, it would seem impossible to be able to increase a project speed through force alone. It's not impossible, but it requires increasing amounts of energy from you and your team. It requires more team members, more resources – more, more, and a little more.

THERE IS A BETTER WAY

Over the next few chapters, you will learn what a better way could be. This was a great basis to start from. You learned that Isaac Newton describes three laws that largely define your understanding of how motion works. His first law defines the qualities of force, the second defines how to quantify force, and the third identifies that there isn't an isolated force in the universe.

This applies to your projects and people simply. In the first law, you can now understand that projects and people are unique in motion and have qualities to the force they bring to the co-creation of the project. You understand, in the second law, that increasing acceleration requires increasing its force or decreasing the number of forces in opposition (the drag), and finally, you understand that you cannot make an isolated choice regarding the project that doesn't have an equal and opposite effect as well.

This all seems logical, but it was never explained to me

when I started in the business world. I was never told to increase my momentum of success; it might have been an underlying assumption, but I didn't realize how interacting on a day-to-day basis impacted my momentum so significantly, nor did I understand how significant that moment was to my thoughts and behaviors.

I love knowing now that momentum is controllable and something that should be leveraged as often as possible. It's far easier for a heavily-laden train to switch tracks to a new path at the right juncture than to stop, back up, and move to another track because it missed the turnoff. This is identical to your project and people momentum. Finding the appropriate path switch means you can alter course without altering momentum, and, in doing this, you never pay the penalty of unsettling the contents of the train as you stop and the equal and opposite reaction is minimized, since the momentum wasn't stopped, the course was just altered.

This is the best path for changing the people and the projects in your lives to new paths. You need to find the switch in the tracks that allows you to seamlessly move from one track to another without pain and without the penalty of stopping. It can be a beautiful experience, or it can be a brutal train wreck. Both have value, but I believe you are looking for the beautiful experience where you accelerate your projects by finding the switch to the new path with ease and with your momentum intact. Why else would you be reading this book?

The more I've realized this aspect, the more fun it is to play with. It's confining in some sense, but caveats are always freeing in that they create definition of the solution, and you can now extrapolate that the problem will create the solution at the same time, based on Newton's third law. It's the equal and opposite action, right? You just need to learn how to find and tune into the solution instead of the problem.

Thus far, I've worked through high-level concepts on how the laws of motion might apply to your projects and people situations – sort of…okay, not much at all. Let's examine this from a different perspective.

SAME CONCEPTS, A DIFFERENT PERSPECTIVE

Newton's laws essentially say that an object will remain in motion unless a force acts upon it, and that force is the product of the object's mass and the accelerations acting on that object. This means that evidence for your project's success comes from your observation of the change in motion of the project's components. You look for outcomes as a result of the energy spent, the force applied, and determine if you feel it was worth it or not. Something I will discuss in Chapter 5 is the concept of kinetic energy and another concept called mass/energy equivalency, which, quickly stated, means that mass and energy are different states of the same thing. Kinetic energy is the energy of an object because it is in motion, so objects gain mass as they go faster because their kinetic energy increases.

Quick recap – making an object move faster means that its mass goes up, and as the mass goes up, it requires more energy to move. Projects work in similar ways; the faster they move, the larger they get, and more energy is required to accelerate them further.

Force gives empirical evidence in this physical world. It is the way to evaluate if anything has happening – if it's moved. Empirical evidence is considered how we evaluate the universe through science. It is done through empiricism, and through empirical evidence of change. "Empirical" is an adjective meaning based on, concerned with, or verifiable by observation or experience rather than theory or pure logic, meaning you must see the result of a force, a movement, or a change.

Projects work on the same principle; the more evidence you want to see toward the results of your efforts, the more force or empirical evidence you look to experience. It also works in similar ways with people in your lives or projects. You expect a certain amount of empirical evidence of their contribution, or some show of the force they bring to your collective experience. In both cases, you traditionally try to accelerate the project and people by moving them faster or applying more force to the situation. You hire more resources, create more processes, have more meetings, send more emails, and ask for more communication to show more continual evidence of our collective desire to move faster. It's awesome, but it's important to realize that these attempts to increase speed result in a similar behavior that you experience through Newton's laws of motion. The increase in acceleration increases the mass, resulting in more and more force needing to be applied faster and faster.

The answer is, quite simply, not to apply more force but instead to find relief from the resistance. You understand from the formula that, if force equals mass multiplied by acceleration, and you were to decrease the mass or decrease the forces of friction or resistance to the mass, you would accelerate with the same amount of force.

TYPES OF RESISTANCE

What kind of resistance do you create for yourself and your teammates that you have the power to alleviate? You create stories about why things are the way they are, why people act the way they do, how competent they are, and how lousy they might be. In the world, as of late, you might even complain that now you are remote and that is the problem;

you say that remote work created barriers that aren't possible to overcome. You create obstacles for yourself and obstacles for your teams. You create and hold onto notions of how things are, and these notions invariably create resistance for how things become. This resistance is the drag you create on the projects and people in your experience. You tell stories about their success or lack thereof. You tell stories about how you do not have enough resources or how a business unit is too fickle and constantly changes direction. Any of these stories are just more resistance to the desire to speed the project or person up.

What should you do? You'll learn more in Chapters 6 and 7 regarding why this works, but for now, the fastest way to increase the speed of the projects and the people working in your experience is to decrease your resistance to their success. This is also known as changing the story you tell. Change it; make it a successful story. At the least, make it a story you tell that isn't demeaning or depowering.

For example, you are on a team of ten people across a few sites. Most people work in isolated groups local to the site and then come together once a week in a video conference with the other teams and line up the work between everyone. There is a fair amount of complaints across the sites about who does what work and if the other teams work all the time. This isn't always ideal as you've accepted before; it creates areas where you are identifying various work resources that must work together because they are at the same site. You all tell yourself this is better for various reasons.

This team is a technical team and delivers periodically. A global pandemic and completely unforeseen circumstances occur, leading to the business moving all workers to work-from-home. Now, you've come to a new circumstance and new problems. There are plenty of choices here and lots to possibly complain about. There are many possibilities to hook our resistance. On the other hand, there are so many positives to it too. You could focus on the positives instead of feeling the resistance. You could find relief in the fact that you live in a modern world and the suite of tools available for remote working is incredible – the best at any point in human history. You could find relief in video conference technologies that are magical in nature in bringing faces and voices together across vast distances of space-time. You could find relief in being freed from the constraint of needing to find localized workers because now everybody is on equal footing. You could find relief in describing how the team succeeded before and will succeed again. You could find relief in the new constraints in the working environment, for constraints can always lead to creative freedom once embraced.

Additionally, you could find relief in all the thoughts that came before that make the internet work and how resilient the internet is for humanity. You could find relief in the magic of transporting and converting light into data and all that has come from this concept. You could find relief in the peace of your home working environment compared to the chaos of an office. You could find relief in embracing a more flexible working schedule because you're saving time in your life from commuting. You could find relief in how amazing the world is that created keyboards and data entry; imagine the internet as a culminating collection of keystrokes, and imagine all of that abundance that has built the internet to what it is today.

All of these thoughts feel so much better and offer relief to the resistance you were creating with the stories about how disempowered you were in this new place and time. It's often the easiest thing in the world to do. The easiest way is to be more general with your thoughts. Instead of focusing on a specific problem, like remote work as a barrier, you can find a more general perspective about how amazing the world is that allows the remote work efficiency that you have today. Often, you can tell by the words you are using how general you are being and how much momentum is going with your narrative. The question words of "why" and "what" build momentum from a general place. The question words of "when," "who," "how," and "where," are much more specific, carry with them more momentum, and if they are raised too soon, will bring more resistance. You can see how focusing on the individual that needs to deliver task twenty-three on Friday by the meeting with the client who is expected to close the contract has a lot of momentum to it. The generalized perspective might be that you want to sign the client because you want to help them succeed. This is more generalized and carries less momentum and resistance. The added details will always make their way into our equation at the proper time as you allow the energy to flow, and when they come in at the proper time, they accelerate the process. When they are raised too soon, they slow it down with more momentum.

You can find relief in just about anything, or you can find resistance in just about anything. It's important to realize what our point of focus is, and what the narrative you tell for all the various aspects of your life matter is. For, as you have learned in this chapter, and as Newton described it, resistance to change in motion is the nature of your physical mass, your matter.

Resistance isn't bad; it's stabilizing. Imagine how crazy a world without resistance or friction would be for us physically. Everything would be sloshing around and wiggly and wonderfully unable to do anything. You need resistance; in fact, you love it. It's the foundation of our physicality. You just need to realize when it serves you and when it doesn't.

Does it serve you in this project? Does it serve you in your interaction with your coworker? Are you resistant to your self-leadership? When I discuss energy flow in Chapters 8 and 9, you will come back to these questions.

USING RESISTANCE

This entire process is with you constantly. It's a part of you as a human being, like your breath. You inhale, creating an internal tension, and then you exhale, releasing that tension. In breathing, it's important to know how much tension to have so you don't pass out or explode. You feel it physically. This is the same way you feel resistance physically in projects and your interactions with other people, and it's equally as important to honor these indicators too.

If you release the resistance to your project, you make them move faster. Your focus on those outputs is an interesting part of this experience. You can create resistance just in your focus on looking for something to go faster and looking for that empirical evidence of movement.

Here's how that works. In focusing on going faster, the actual focus is on the result of what going faster would deliver, so in fact, the focus is on the lack of what is presently delivered. Follow? The resistance you created in this process, with your expectation and evaluation for the empirical results, is focus on the manifested evidence things moved faster. The resistance you create isn't in the project in this aspect; it's in energy flow within you, which is something that I discuss more in Chapter 8. The way you feel this resistance is in the narrative of the story you tell about any subject. As mentioned in the preceding paragraphs, much of this focus on the problem creates resistance to the solution, which was the reaction to the action.

The laws of motion are incredible for the simplicity they

define your physical interactions. Even in the early stages of this description, it's easy to see how they can also apply to the experiences brought to the projects and people in your lives. You can learn to accelerate your projects by finding relief to your resistance. You find that resistance comes out in the stories you tell about things, either outwardly or through an internal dialogue. At this point, it's probable that you have been telling the stories for so long, you can't even tell that they don't feel good to tell, aren't serving you, and could and should change to a new perspective.

In the next chapters, I will discuss more about how this works. For now, it's enough to understand that your projects slow down largely from the narrative of the story you tell, which is an indicator of the current beliefs of the accumulated resistance with the project and people. Finding relief is easy; I shared some alternative views that might bring some relief to the example story. Maybe it will help you find relief in some of your stories too.

I love the consistency of this effect. I love knowing that it's not about the force I apply, but rather about the relief to resistance I can bring that accelerates the project – every time. Now, if only it were as easy as just having one project and not multiple or many different relationships accelerating.

Next, let's talk through relational movement and how our relationships and perspectives alter so much. Before you do, I'll quickly recap all that was learned in this chapter. You learned about Newton's three laws of motion – force, momentum, acceleration, and mass. I then shared how you can create or release resistance by changing your question words and that there isn't just one force, they always happen in equal and opposite pairs. In the next chapter, you will take this concept of pairs and understand how it impacts your relationships. You will learn that you have so much control over that perspective and what that means to your experience. It is important to build positive momentum and not increase resistance. Increasing positive momentum will always increase the speed over time as well. You feel this in the resistance of the project or your resistance to deal with or talk to certain people. It is relational, it's relative, and it's the next piece in this understanding.

5

RELATING PERSPECTIVE AND DESIRE TO PROJECT OBSERVATION

"When you are courting a nice girl, an hour seems like a second. When you sit on a red-hot cinder, a second seems like an hour. That's relativity."

— ALBERT EINSTEIN

In the early 1900s, Albert Einstein shared his theory of relativity with the world, and it became the dominant way humans explained their physical experience in time and space for over one hundred years. I'm not going to even try to explain the math in this book; there exists boundless amounts of content on these subjects already.

I'd like to mention that Einstein came to his conclusions largely from playing thought games. One of these games was to imagine what it would be like to ride a light wave in the universe across space. He came to describe the universe with the simplistic beauty of a co-creation between the speed of light squared and mass. Mass, as described in the previous chapters, is described as the resistance to change in motion. It is effectively a value for matter or material (particles) that make up a physical body of mass. It is the product of the volume and density of an object, and again and for emphasis, mass is resistance to change in motion. The speed of light is the distance light travels in a second; I will keep it defined at a higher level of 187k miles per second. It is the ultimate speed limit in the universe, and anything with mass can't exceed it or even go as fast as it. The speed of light is the speed that massless particles radiate into space, while radiation is the emission of energy as electromagnetic waves or moving subatomic particles. Radiation also means to be divergent from a central point.

Einstein's equation elegantly describes the co-creation of resistance to movement and the maximum movement possible in our space-time reality. From this elegance and simplicity, we've come to understand a great deal of our universe, and you will understand how you relate to your projects and people even more because of it.

The theory of relativity gave us several qualitative experiences that you can understand from all the quantified mathematics that reinforced this theory for a century. Let's go through those takeaways and relate them back to how they influence the speed you can get your projects and people to move too. I promise it's all relative.

Einstein initially took the inertial frame of reference that Newton had and decided you didn't have that inertial frame; there wasn't a fixed reference in the universe – there wasn't a time when all things weren't accelerating in relation to all things. In Chapter 4, you basked in the simplicity of discussing the motion of your projects and people in them more individually. I didn't discuss how they interacted with each other, how they related to each other, or how your interaction with them influences them. It was all about resistance, acceleration, force, and empirical evidence.

RELATIVE QUALITIES

Perhaps one of the most significant understandings that Einstein shared was that time itself is relative to the observer. There is a concept of "time dilation," which describes how, the faster an object moves, the slower it measures time passing relative to a stationary observer. This is kind of mind-bending at first, but eventually you begin to understand it; the more resistance you have to the speed of light, the more time you create. Taking this quickly back to how it would work with what I described with Newton's laws in Chapter 4, the less resistance you feel, the faster you move, and the less time you experience. How crazy is that? Seriously, think about it; the less resistance you have, the faster you go *and* the less time you experience. There is so much power in this concept, but I don't want to go too far into it now when there are several other qualitative understandings from relativity that also matter.

Humans understand that time is relative to the speed a mass is moving relative to an observer. You also learned from Einstein's theory that length is relative. The faster an object moves, the shorter it appears relative to its direction of motion compared to a slower-moving object. It's a subtle effect that, of course, is experienced as you try to speed up your project and people. Consider the faster you make a project go, the shorter it appears, yet the slower it goes, the bigger and more awkward it appears. This is all about the resistance I started describing in the previous chapter on motion and Newton's second law.

From Einstein's theory, you also understand that mass and energy are equivalent. That is, they are different manifestations of the same thing, which means that a quantity of mass times the speed of light squared is equal to a quantity of energy. This is known for certain because it's how and why bombs explode. The destruction of tiny amounts of mass releases massive amounts of energy. You can see our projects in this way too, based on the amount of spent energy invested in building a project. If the project was also destroyed, that input energy would radiate outward explosively to all aspects that project touched and the people involved. This might be a bit dramatic, but I've experienced these explosive results of a project's destruction on several occasions.

Next up is kinetic energy, which is the energy a body possesses just because it's in motion. The same object resting will have less mass than the same object moving fast because of the mass-energy equivalency.

Does this make sense? These three concepts I briefly mentioned in the previous chapter, mass and energy equivalency and kinetic energy, are the reason projects require more and more force or energy to continue to accelerate faster.

There are several types of kinetic energy that science reports – mechanical, electrical, thermal, radiant, and sound. There are also types of potential energy, which are chemical, nuclear, gravitational, and elastic. Again, this will be relevant later.

As you briefly learned in the previous chapter, as you speed up mass, it increases the kinetic energy of the object and therefore the mass, and mass is defined as resistant to changing motion, thus, the more mass increases the more the mass resists increasing further. The more you increase the speed, the more energy is required to move it. This is the why Einstein believed that the speed of light is the barrier in our physical reality, and that nothing with mass can exceed the speed of light because it would have to build up to an infinite amount of energy necessary to move an object with an infinite amount of mass to the speed of light.

You also learned that space and time are part of one

continuum called space-time. Space-time is a grid of three dimensions with a fourth dimension considered to be time.

Relativity also explained where gravity came from. It explained that since space-time was a grid, that mass would warp this space-time continuum and create things called gravity wells. A gravity well is the pull that a large body exerts because it has warped more of space-time. The more the mass of this body, the more it creates a deeper well. You see these concepts of gravity wells in the solar system quite easily. The sun has the largest gravity well, and all the planets orbit around it via paths of least resistance, or paths of most energy returned. Each planet has respective gravity wells that create these paths of least resistance for other masses to orbit around. All mass warps space-time for all other mass through gravity. The Law of Gravity is effectively the manager of physical matter in this way.

Gravity wells create another concept that is super interesting for your relating to projects and people. Consider this: when humanity wants to put an object in space, we've learned that you must accelerate that object to what is known as escape velocity. This is defined as the lowest velocity (speed and direction) a body must have in order to escape the gravitational attraction of a particular object. Once this gravity well has been established to your projects and people, and it has most certainly been established, it has its own escape velocity for new ideas, new concepts, and new paths of the project. They must have enough velocity to escape the pull of the gravity of the project's mass. Let's play with this a little before you move on because I think it's important and, of course, relative.

In the project space, you always have preconceived notions and expectations of the project's success and challenges. These preconceived notions are a type of velocity that is either working with the gravity of the project or against it.

Let's play with it a bit. You have had a project running for a couple of months, and it has a sustained gravity around it and it's collaborating and cooperating components. Most components are orbiting in the expected ways and flowing. Some are challenging, but most are doing well and therefore remain unbothered. However, Sam, the newest member of the team, has an idea of how to improve the performance of the project. He brings it to the team during the team meeting, and, as expected, the idea is received but ultimately put down because it is a change to the project with a new workflow, and, at this point, nobody wants to allow the changes or adapt to the workflow. How can Sam, who is convinced of the right fit for his idea, make it impactful to the project? In my experience. he must put in additional effort and focus on this change he believes will improve things. He must build his momentum of this on his own until it has enough stability and gravity to pull in other resources. He must supply his own type of escape velocity to his idea so that it can break free of the gravitational pull and accepted paths of least resistance of all the current components of the project. Sam will succeed with this as he works on his idea and formulates it more, actualizing more and more of it until some additional components start to orbit around his new ideas too and begin building momentum. Eventually, there will be sufficient momentum from his efforts that his idea will break free. It will achieve escape velocity, and the project team will accept this improvement without issues because it has found a path toward orbiting the project's gravity in a beneficial way.

The final quality of space-time that you've learned from the theory of relativity is something called a gravity lens. This is a concept where you, as an observer of the universe, point a telescope across space and time to a distant object. As the light from this object travels across space-time, it is warped by all the matter/mass/gravity that exists in the path between you, the observer, and the light's source. This results in duplicate images in the telescope, and it can also be used to magnify light in a lensing effect. In a project space, this lensing creates confusion about goals and targets because you see multiple endpoints when there is just one. It can also warp the perspective of the project by magnifying an aspect of a problem or person that distorts what is wanted and the real goal.

RELATING TO MORE

Einstein gave concepts to understand how to relate to the physical world. He did it with physics and math, but you can take these same concepts and apply them to how you understand your world. For the book, specifically, you will learn at how it influences your projects and people in your life, and of course, ultimately what this means to the speed of these projects and their success.

Let's review – mass in these equations is defined as resistance to change in motion and a product of density and volume in space-time. It is easy to tell me that projects and people aren't mass in the way that Einstein or Newton described it, but I disagree; the base definition of mass is resistance to change in motion. Projects and people are, by this definition, without doubt, mass of some sort. They all resist changes in motion. They all want to follow the paths of least resistance in this physical world. Why? They want this because all the objects want as much energy as possible. Paths of least resistance are exactly that – orbits where planets utilize the warped curvature of space-time to orbit larger mass without using excess energy.

Have you ever noticed how projects and people orbit around similar ways? The most influential person in a team generally creates a gravity well around them that leads others to follow their orbit. This might be useful, or it might be horrible. It depends on the dynamic, but it will always occur. It's the nature of mass in space-time; you can't avoid it. Does this give a different perspective of the quote I started the book with from Eisenhower? What kind of leader do you relate to personally or in a group? What kind of influence and gravity do you create?

I like to think of Einstein's theory of relativity, as I mentioned earlier, as one of co-creation. The understanding of the behavior of time matters for an observer. The observer is co-creating the experience with the observed. This is so important to understand.

We, as mass, co-create our experience through our resistance to our changes in motion. You identify with this resistance as our life experiences and as who you are. The resistance is our struggle with change; they are the things you've fought with and the things you feel define you – and they totally do define you, or one aspect of you, and it's through this aspect that you become aware of how your motion in this universe is influencing and affecting all the motions around us.

If you think about Einstein's model just a little bit, it's simple and beautiful. It says that resistance to movement, and the most movement possible, co-create to give us space-time and everything that comes from it.

What, really, is space? It's required when two particles exist uniquely. When there was only one particle, it was singular. When two particles existed, there was a concept of the stuff in-between the particles making them distinct, and where these particles existed, they had locality in relationship with one another and they had awareness of their uniqueness. This locality and this space between are what you define as space. Space is dimensionality; it's relationship-based. Even objects are relationally based on their volume and density of the space they consume.

Time was the co-created result of these two particles existing in different points of this new space. The distance between these two particles relative to how quickly they were changing locality became a measure you referred to as time. Everything is about co-creation because everything is relational.

APPLIED RELATIVITY

Let's consider what you now know about these laws and apply that to our project and people situations again; after all, you did come here for help with projects.

In the last chapter, you first learned that going faster requires us to accelerate mass. In this chapter, you learned that, as you increase that speed, kinetic energy is gained, and in turn, mass is gained. As more energy is added to increase the speed, the mass continues to increase. As this mass increases, so will its gravity well. As the gravity well increases, the mass influences more and more objects, which are also influenced by this increasing gravity well.

You see, even without directly being able to calculate how the mass of our projects changes as you increase its delivery, you can understand how its influence and its resistance to change also increases. Humans know that, at the speed of light, time is not experienced, and because of time dilation, the faster something moves, the less time it will experience relative to something moving slower. It is often this result that messes up your intuition about your projects. Why is this? It is a matter of perspective. You as the observer of the project are also influencing your awareness of the time related to the project based on your observations. I will describe in Chapter 6, the next chapter, how time and the expansion of your awareness are linked and the impact on your perspective. Then in Chapter 7, I will describe even more ways that the influence you have on the project and people in your life is a direct reflection of this awareness and your current focus. Until this reflective quality is understood, most people operate on the concept that seeing is believing. Once you understand how your reality reflects your awareness of it, more and more believing will be seeing.

I tried to describe how the real answer to increasing project and people delivery is to remove resistance. You understand this more now because of relativity. You understand that, as you increase speed, mass increases, and increasing of mass means that you need to apply more force to go faster. Well, the side effect is that, the more resistance you can remove, the more resistance you find relief in feeling, the faster things can accelerate too.

In fact, from Einstein's equation, it states that anything with mass behaves this way. Anything that is resistant to change in motion behaves this way, so you know the easiest way to accelerate is to release tension – to release the resistance. In the coming chapters, you will learn how to do this more effectively; for now, just understand that there is a reason for it.

Resistance is the thing that slows you down. Perhaps better said, it's the thing that keeps you from going fast. It's the thing that led to the stability of your space-time continuum, and it's the thing that is used to create contrast so you can identify more. You love resistance; you physically are resistance.

I began describing a situation in Chapter 4 about wanting to move a project faster and how to find relief in the process to help it move faster. You can now begin to understand more how your past experiences create the resistance to your future experiences. This is relative to how you work with your projects, teams, and life in general.

CO-CREATED REALITIES

> *"Life is a series of natural and spontaneous changes.*
> *Don't resist them – that only creates sorrow.*
> *Let reality be reality.*
> *Let things flow naturally forward in whatever way they like."*
>
> — LAO TZU

Einstein described the universe in terms of relationships, and I will describe the universe in terms of co-creation. From Einstein's equation, you have an understanding of what $E=M*C^2$ means, but it also gives two different types of co-creation. First, the co-creation of our mass-energy equivalency, which gives us our subjective reality, and second, the co-creation of mass and the speed of light squared, which gives us our objective reality.

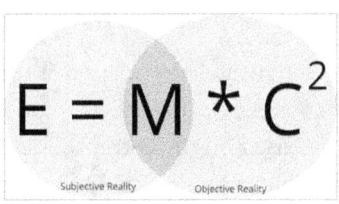

Energy and mass equivalency is the first co-creation, and it defines your unique subjective reality in that it is the reality of one observer or mass and is composed of that observer's emotions, experiences, and vibrations collectively. It is created by mass-energy equivalency as defined by Einstein's Theory of Relativity. You then can see an objective reality in that it includes the other aspect of the equations ($M*C^2$). Society determined that objective reality is what matters. It is the reality that exists outside the individual mind; it is what is referred to as "real."

Everything that exists in the objective reality has a co-created relationship with all that exists in the subjective reality. The observer has a perspective and their own translations of what occurs in the objective reality. Historically, most projects and teams tried to minimize the subjective reality because it is unknown and appears to be an uncontrollable variable. Yet, the perceptions that exist in the subjective reality are the individual's beliefs and understandings of how they fit into the objective reality. It's critical that, within your projects and people situations, you honor the subjective reality for what it is, an individualized reflection of the resistance to their perception of objective reality.

By honoring this subjective reality more, you can come to more understanding that the resistance is causing your slowness in your projects and people involvement. Remember, mass is the resistance to change in motion and it is interchangeable with energy, so the subjective perspective is one about how much energy is flowing and how much is being resisted.

Let me state that again – any subjective reality is based on the present resistance to a change in motion of that individual object. It is based on the current thought patterns that are defined in the individual by the individual. The thought patterns come from their history of experience and failures related to this topic and all others they have experienced and built relationships upon. The subjective reality is the source of your narrative stories about success and failure. It's the place you find your beliefs and expectations, and it's the place you find your joy or your horror; it's all about resistance to moving.

It's crazy, right? Not unless you define logical as crazy. As you start to understand how you create your realities, projects and people naturally align to a base understanding, an awareness of the essence of the interactions.

You are matter, which is mass, and mass resists changes in motion. Momentum and force from Newton's laws describe how motion behaves and how you can speed it up or not. From Einstein's work, you now understand that you have a speed limit in the universe, and as you speed up toward it as mass, you get more massive, and it requires more and more energy to keep speeding up. Momentum helps with that process by continuing to build speed in a specific direction, generally utilizing the force of gravity. This direction you can see as a path for your projects. The more you keep on the same path, the more you can increase that momentum. The increased momentum makes changes to the motion of the object more and more difficult. Momentum on earth with objects is easily understood with trains and hills. Momentum of thought is less easy to grasp, yet nonetheless is still there.

As your projects grow, they resist changes to movement. It's the nature of them. More people are involved, more resources are required, more time is necessary to discuss, more value is created, and more things start to orbit around the gravity well of the project. You now understand that these other objects naturally want to orbit the mass of the project and are resistant to the change of the project itself. They all will find a path of least resistance to their fit in the project.

You can also utilize these paths of least resistance to go faster. Consider how satellites and spaceships in movies utilize the gravity well of planets to accelerate and then launch the ship further and faster into space. Imagine if there was a way of doing this with your people and projects – a way of keeping people moving from one project (gravity well) to another without losing momentum, but increasing it. Is this possible? Of course it is, but you need details in the coming chapters to pull this all together more.

Let's discuss the gravity lens briefly too. What if you view the business health through multiple project failure lenses? This gravity of the project, or people's interactions, is significant. You might not realize how you orbit these previous thoughts. You might not recognize the stories of resistance you have built up over time. You are aware of it, but often grow accustomed to it make it feel normal. Nonetheless, you use these various gravity wells of resistance to see through and they create the lens you define your current success and failures by. At this point, these current thoughts are indicators of resistance and the narratives that you created from these past experiences.

With each interaction, you co-create a new interaction and redefine the relationship between the observer and the observed. You can take these old stories of resistance into the stories and co-create more resistance, or you can take these old stories and find the relief to the resistance I described in Chapter 4. You can find relief to the resistance, and as you do, you co-create a new situation with less resistance and therefore more speed and less time. It is possible through just a subtle difference in perspective.

Both the laws of motion from Newton and the theory of relativity from Einstein have mass's resistance to changes in motion as a core understanding. Newton saw it as resistance to change in motion and Einstein's theory saw it more as the relationship of the motion to other resistant motions. Matter and mass are resistance. As discussed in Chapter 4, this resistance gives stability, but you must be aware of when it serves you and when it no longer serves you.

This means that you, as mass, create your own resistance

to changes in motion. Your resistance comes out as the narrative you tell about any specific subject, but is always an indicator of the resistance you have active on any specific subject.

FROM ANOTHER PERSPECTIVE

You have relationships with your projects, and these relationships are unique to you. The projects exists in both objective realities and the subjective realities of each person observing. These observations then lead to additional observations based on the preceding understanding. Basically, you expect things to evolve a certain way, and your observations almost always align with that expectation.

Time dilation teaches an important concept. The faster something is going, the less time is experienced, while the slower something goes, the more time is experienced. This is all relative, of course, to an observer whose unique relative observations are unique aspects of awareness in the universe. This observer is a unique focal point where the product of light radiation and accumulated resistance to that radiation produces uniqueness in all the universe. That is, only this one aspect has its unique relationship with all that it observed.

What does this mean regarding your projects? Well, it means that what you observe and focus on will determine how much resistance is felt and therefore how fast you can go, for in having less resistance you always go faster under the same amount or less force. Generally, with projects and work situations you observe, you build your relationships with projects based on previous success, based on the team members working on the project with you, and based on their previous success in relation to your perspective. It all seems quite complex, and I suppose it is, but it's also incredibly simple. All things have relationships with all other things they observe, and the relationships formed are eternal, for all subsequent thoughts are related through concepts of these relations.

The amount the relationship influences the other things are based on the amount of resistance involved and the orbits of those things. In a real way, you could see how you've created orbits of thoughts and patterns in your life around those masses and concepts that mean the most to you. The more something matters and the more focus and resistance to change in your life, the more its gravity well increases and therefore the more things orbit around it. Further, the more this gravity well increases, the more it influences the light around it, warping more and more perception around this concept. It's a truly fascinating, and I admit it doesn't play into the classical usage of relativity in physics. I will explain more in the coming chapters regarding how this physical understanding of relativity in our space-time continuum works with these more than physical concepts, such as projects.

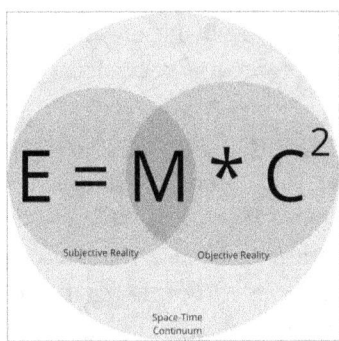

For now, it's so incredible to understand that all our physical space-time experience is summarized with two formulas, $E=M*C^2$ and $F=M*A$. The second comes from Newton's second law of motion and was discussed in the previous chapter. Force gives the empirical evidence that something happened, something moved in your space-time experience, and relativity gives an understanding that all that empirical evidence is relative to who and what observed it and how much resistance to the speed of light they had when they made the observation. The first time I realized this, I found it astoundingly profound.

The amount of resistance of the observer is always relative to the amount of resistance in the observation. I will explain this more in later chapters and say it in many other ways, but it is a crucial understanding in releasing the resistance of the current projects to their higher speed potentials.

One more time – as an observer, your resistance relative to what is observed determines the speed of the observation relative to the objective speed of the occurrence. In other words, how fast the watcher moves determines what is possible to observe of an object of relative speed, or your perceptions of the resistance and success of your projects are relative to project's actual resistance.

Allow me, at this still early stage, to provide an example that will help you build more relationships with this understanding. I remember early in my career often feeling different states of being overwhelmed or in control. At this point in my career. I never considered it had anything to do with my mood or the speed of my being. I believed it was the outward experience that defined me. In the projects I felt empowered by or owned directly, I always felt a sense of interest and pride in them. Almost all aspects of the projects felt simple, possible, and deliverable. In the projects that I was forced into and did not like the project management, I did not feel the same level of interest. I felt forced to do certain things and overwhelmed much of the time. At the time, I complained it was the project leadership or the toolset or company management or anything else I could find that left me feeling better. In this perspective of the world, the seeing is believing perspective, it always felt better to blame something else when you aren't experiencing the results you desire.

What I've described in this chapter thus far means that my resistance to this project, the management, you name it, was high and therefore, I moved slower in relation to the actual speed of the project. My overwhelmed being was caused by my focus on the lack of everything I wanted more of and how I didn't like what I had. These are higher resistance perspectives and therefore slowed my perceptions down. Knowing what you now know about time dilation, this slowing down made everything else I perceived seem faster. These faster aspects experienced less time than my slower perspective. The result was that I felt overwhelmed when I focused in this way. When I did not focus in this way and focused on anything satisfying, my overwhelmed state faded. It faded because, as you will learn in Chapter 8, this feeling of satisfaction was coming into a less resistant state. In this less resistant state, my being moved faster, and I could not be overwhelmed. I felt up to speed with the project and people in it. Is this starting to make a bit more sense? Are you understanding more and more that your perspective means everything for your experience?

AWARENESS AND RELATIONAL FLOW

Relativity is interesting, as is understanding time dilation. Have you ever played sports and found yourself in the flow? Time slows down relative to you as you speed up. Thoughts and movement are connected and instant; it's fluid, elegant, and timeless. This is because, relative to the things going on around you at this time, you found less resistance. It is time dilation in your experience. The phrase, "a watched pot never boils," is an example of this time dilation in your reality. The boredom you feel in the slowness of being forced to focus on something like a tea kettle feels painful relative to the excitement of scoring a winning goal in the game. This boredom is created out of your perspective relative to the experience of resistance from doing what isn't wanted, which causes the experience of time to be even greater, hence the pot never boiling. Of course, it's likely to boil at the same speed it always has if tested, but the experience of watching it and waiting is one of boredom and drag to your energy and makes it feel like time takes forever.

It is the awareness and co-creation that provides the experiences and gives the opportunity to be observed. This awareness is central to your understanding of anything, for it is your awareness of it that makes it so. Your awareness of the relationships of resistance to changes in movement is perhaps the core understanding of all things, and you just experience the expansion from the process evolving eternally.

Think about how much resistance to various aspects of the project's success you currently have. Think of all the stories about how difficult something was and how grateful it is to be past this hard part. Think of all those stories again about the difficulties in working from home and how it was going to only increase the problems. This is all about your relationship with and perspective on those things.

It's fun to break it down to something easy to discuss, like resistance or allowance. Effectively, planets allow themselves to follow the paths of least resistance to the orbits they have. Think of how crazy the universe would be if these paths of least resistance didn't exist. It's an amusing thought game for me. Without paths of least resistance to follow, planets wouldn't orbit; there would be no order to the universe as you know it. Assuming in this crazy world planets could still form, some might go in straight lines, some might travel in triangles or square patterns or not at all. In this space-time reality, paths of least resistance do exist and they are consistent. The larger the resistance to change in motion, the larger the well around it; the larger the well around it, the more of it will impact the mass around it, and the more space-time it will warp. These wells create the stability for more and more to relate to them. They become central to the experience of so much more.

This is the same desire you share of your projects and building your teams. It is to build stability for so much to come after; it is not to build the slowness and resistance to changes in motion. This is the awareness you must have going forward so that you create these relationships in everything and anything you do. They are enduring relationships of co-creation, and they are largely based on the speed and resistance of the observers and the observations at time of co-creation. Once you have the awareness, as you will learn in the next chapter, you will be permanently changed by it and all future perspectives and experiences will incorporate it in some way. The awareness is individualized, and it's through this individual awareness that you lead others by the example of your own clarity.

Speed up the projects and people in your life by feeling less resistance. Speed up the people and processes in your life by creating less resistance through focus on flow. It's all about awareness, co-creation, and how you use your awareness to co-create your relationships. Now, what is awareness?

6

AWARENESS OF PROBLEMS AND POSSIBILITIES

"A man's mind is stretched by a new idea or sensation, and never shrinks back to its former dimensions."

— OLIVER WENDELL HOLMES SR.

In Chapter 4, I discussed the laws of motion. You learned that there are three laws, and the concepts they provide helped to understand how movement in the physical world works. In Chapter 5, you then learned how this movement you learned about is all relative to the movement the observer has of it. I applied the concepts of resistance to projects and people as concepts of mass, for they have resistance to changes in motion. This, of course, isn't aligned with the pure nature of physics and is my interpretation of the laws and behaviors of these concepts, and by the end of the book, you'll understand why. In this chapter, I will continue with that analytical extrapolation as I consider what the observer is and why this understanding will improve your projects' performance.

Conscious means to be aware, and self-conscious means

to be aware of self. Self-awareness means that you have a notion of your place – the place of self – in reference to all other-selves or aspects of your universe. It is that broad, for Einstein's understood qualities of relativity rely on co-creation to establish the relationships and therefore two separate points of observational creation. These are two separate points of consciousness, for there are two separate aspects that are now in awareness of their relationship with one another. It's quite simple in these concepts but mind-boggling in-depth, for you are each the accumulated awareness of our relationships, and all-that-is is accumulated awareness of all relationships.

If you look at Einstein's equation one more time, $E=M*C^2$, you can understand that energy equals mass times the speed of light squared. Where or what is the observer in that reference? Is it the light, the mass, or the energy?

Humans define ourselves as living in the objective space-time reality because you are physical; you are mass and matter.

Where is the consciousness of this, the awareness of this physical existence, or the awareness of self? It's missing from the equation. The results rely on points of consciousness to have relationships with one another, but awareness and consciousness are explicitly removed from our understanding of matter. Concepts that surround the mind and thoughts lead science to tell a narrative about how it's dissimilar and can't be modeled like physics models space-time. That might have been, but I believe in the next two chapters, I'll bridge this gap more so you can understand how your awareness is consistently understandable.

MASS AND MATTER

Mass is resistant to change in motion, and it is also referred to as matter. Matter is the generic reference to mass, and mass is the specific reference to a quantifiable number of particles making up a system, a body, or an object, as discussed in Chapter 5. You know this definition of mass. It is resistant to change in motion and is defined as the product of volume and density. You, as a physical being, have a volume and a density in space and time. Just as the projects and people in our lives have some level of resistance to change in motion, they also have some amount of intangible volumes and densities as you think about their relationships with other aspects of your life.

The definition of matter is, "physical substance in general, as distinct from mind and spirit; (in physics) that which occupies space and possesses rest mass, especially as distinct from energy." I find this so fascinating. Our shared definition of matter explicitly excludes energy, mind, and spirit as part of our composition. You know that energy and mass are interchangeable, and the co-creation of mass and the speed of light squared has co-created your space-time continuum.

However, where are mind and spirit in this equation? They aren't included, yet they are the thing that defines the experience of being in space-time. It's all about the observer and the relationship with what is observed. What is this awareness to these observations and to the changes in perspective? According to that definition of matter, they can't be physical. Energy, mind, and spirit are distinct from matter.

Relativity, as defined by $E=M*C^2$, largely describes how I understand space-time. It is the best and simplest equation to define the physical experience, as one of relations and co-creations. What I think is so interesting is that the definition of matter excludes mind and spirit as physical. They are defined as distinct from the physical world used to calculate our qualities and experiences, although, as I stated in the previous chapter and several times in this chapter, it's all the observation of the various aspects and the relationships formed that makes any of it possible.

If I define the physical world through Einstein's equation, what are the essentials that make up the physical from this understanding?

The physical world is based on limits. You are limited in your physicality. You are limited by how fast you can move, how big your body is, how fast information can travel; and in fact, the concept of mass is a description of the various particles that make up a physical system in increasing stages of complexity. Generally, the more mass, the more complex the underlying structure. These various aspects of mass are what helps you see the limit of one system and the start of another. The limits produce contrast, and contrast enables you to make choices, experience differences, and create preferences.

What else does the equation describe about the physical world? It describes resistance, as mass is resistance to change in motion. This resistance is the stability and structure of your physical world. You need it; you love it. This resistance gives you things to build from and bounce off while making more. It allows you to move and to experience this universe tangibly.

And what else does this equation describe about your physical reality? It describes radiation. The speed of light is the speed of electromagnetic radiation or the speed at which massless particles emanate and travel across a vacuum of space-time.

Now, from these preceding understandings, I can define our physical experience based on three characteristics: limits, resistance, and radiation.

This is awesome, right? I think so, but it gets even more awesome.

NON-PHYSICAL ENVIRONMENT OF MIND AND THOUGHT

If I'm saying that mind and spirit – my awareness – are separate from my physical reality, where do they exist? You know you have a mind and spirit because you are constantly experiencing the result of your awareness and life through their perceptions. If they are distinct from matter and therefore aren't physical, they must be non-physical.

What would a non-physical environment look like?

It would be the inverse of the physical environment, of course. It would be characterized by limitlessness, non-resistance, and the collection of energy. Limitless and nonresistance are easy conclusions to understand. But why collection? Collecting is the opposite of radiating, as illustrated in the following picture. Collection is represented as a spiral/vortex, while radiation is represented by a wave. A wave and a spiral are the same shapes from different perspectives. Non-physically, there is no space to have energy radiate into and through. There is only the non-physical collection of energy that continues to expand and evolve. Why do I represent the non-physical collection as a spiral? Because this is the shape that humans can understand as something that is always increasing and becoming more.

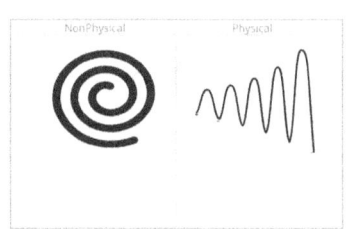

Now, with this understanding, you can define your non-physical environment as one that is limitless, non-resistant, and energy collecting. The following table illustrates the differences:

Non-Physical	Physical
Limitless	Limited
Nonresistant	Resistant
Collecting	Radiating

Am I saying that humans are both non-physical and physical? Yes, I am saying precisely that.

Given the logic I've stepped through to this point, that is exactly the concept I want you to understand. Your mind and spirit are non-physical. Your mass is physical. You are a blend of the two aspects.

I believe that you are co-creating non-physically and physically. The understanding of the laws of motion and relativity still apply, but they apply to the environment in which the experience occurs. The non-physical experience is different than the physical, yet they are reflections of each other.

I believe that everything is the result of co-creation and that the definition of matter, excluding spirit and mind, points to another possible co-creation. As Einstein eloquently described the universe through relational co-creation physically, is it possible to describe the universe through relational co-creation non-physically? Of course, it is possible. I'm about to do it for you.

Oliver Wendel Homes described how the mind stretches to new ideas and in that stretching it does not – and cannot – return to its original dimension. Why not? It cannot, for the mind has grown and expanded beyond that original to become more. This more it has become includes that which it was and the addition of the new expansion; there is no going back. It's collecting, after all. It's in a non-resistant environment; it's limitless.

Let's consider this further. The stretching means that there is a starting point – the awareness before expansion – and an ending point – awareness after expansion. Furthermore, I understand that, once stretched, it remains expanded. Again, your mind operates in a non-physical environment. After stretching – after the expansion – the mind returns to equilibrium, waiting to expand again. This disturbance in the equilibrium of mind creates a vibration, for vibration is disturbance in equilibrium, that is its definition. The expansion and movement of mind create a frequency that this vibration continues to oscillate at because it is nonphysical without resistance. It is this vibration that is aware of itself uniquely from all other vibrations. It has a relationship with where it started and where it expanded to. You, as an observer of this expansion, have a relationship with the expansion as it was and as it is now.

That is a lot to take in, so let me explain it another way. As you live your life physically, you experience contrast in your physical energy flow; this contrast makes you select a preference that is incorporated immediately through the nonphysical expansion of mind and the inclusion of the new awareness. The expansion of mind results in a vibrational frequency of nonphysical movement and is translated as a thought or thought stream, which itself is based on the present relationship with historical translations of similar vibrations. Said yet another way, your previous awareness of your projects and people result in your mind expecting their behavior pattern because you are translating the relationship and vibrational frequencies of these thoughts based on your previous experiences and your relationships to these vibrations, the vibrations that resulted from your ever-expanding awareness of mind. As projects and people change, your mind's concept of these patterns starts to shift to incorporate the expanded perspective of it or resist it and maintain the now old perspective of it.

When I look at it at the most basic place, I believe awareness is at the movement level of the universe itself. Each movement is, and must be, aware of its relationship to the movements around it. Each movement is self-aware and accumulates through levels of complexity just as mass does. It must be that, for the relational part of the universe to work, everything is relational, and the relationships are based on energy flow and awareness of this flow. Everything must be aware of its relationship with everything else to be at all.

I believe that consciousness is at this movement level – not the physical movement level, but the non-physical movement level, which is the level resulting from the expansion of awareness; it is vibrational for reasons I've described already. This is the non-resistant, the limitless, and the collecting energy level of awareness. This is the side that expands to incorporate the new – the stretching of the mind. This is the domain of conscious awareness. Each frequency of vibration is aware of itself as a unique frequency of vibration.

For emphasis and to say this a third way, Oliver Wendel Holmes stated eloquently that the mind expands and doesn't collapse. This means that, after expansion, the mind returns to a state of equilibrium incorporating the non-physical new expansion. In a non-physical world, the expansion is the disturbance of the equilibrium of awareness Holmes was describing. The disturbance results in a vibration, just as it would in classical or quantum mechanical theory when equilibrium is disturbed. It's just that, in a non-physical environment, the vibration is a frequency of energetic expansion that can only increase. With no force or resistance to decrease, it is always additive. The more a mind expands, the more the expansion causes disturbance in equilibrium of mind and the higher a vibrational frequency created from the expansions. Each expansion contains all the energy of the previous expansions, plus the new addition. Each expansion is a movement that is self-contained in relation to what it is and what it is becoming. Each continues to vibrate after expansion. This is quite profound, and I'll continue to explain it more and more. Again, it matters.

NON-PHYSICAL CO-CREATION

"Nothing happens until something moves."

— ALBERT EINSTEIN

Since I believe everything is related to co-creation, I also believe the mind is co-creating. In the previous chapter, I explained how the objective and subjective realities coexist with one another. Now, let's examine how the non-physical world co-creates realities as well.

The collective energy is the opposite of radiation energy. This energy acts in a similar way to the speed of light, except it's not limiting in that same sense. If it was limiting, it would be physical in concept, but it's non-physical, limitless, and a collection of energy. What is the energy that it is collecting? It is collecting conscious energy as you make your preference for the contrasting energy flows of your life. This collection, because it is non-physical and not limited, is a collection of conscious asking of preference from all the physical experience. This energy, and your individualized aspects of it, co-create to give you your experience.

This co-created collected awareness and your individualized expanded aspect creates a continuum of vibration-expansion, and like the physical environment co-created the objective and subjective realities, your non-physical environment co-creates the collective and vibrational realities.

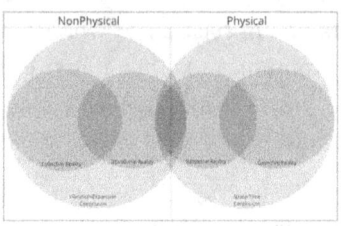

The flow of energy from subjective awareness to the physical objective world is called actualization. You are actualizing the conscious energy into a material object that resists change in motion and has stability. The flow of energy from the non-physical world to the subjective world is called realization, in that you realize what the frequency of vibrational expansion means to you specifically.

Awareness is a nonphysical trait. It's aware of the motions around it, and it's aware of where it is and what it wants next. Awareness is movement that is self-aware as a movement in relation to all other movement. The non-physical environment is one of vibration and expansion. The vibration is a frequency of energetic movement that has expanded the consciousness of all. I've called this consciousness the current of consciousness, for there is only one and it is always the furthest expansion of all consciousness, and it is always the highest order of awareness in the non-physical world. As the highest energy source non-physically, it behaves similarly to the speed of light physically, and just as mass distorts the fabric of space-time, the non-physical movement of your desires distorts the flow of the current of consciousness to you.

The current of consciousness is always at the furthest expansion of all awareness and is always at equilibrium. As new conscious energy is added to the collection, it expands and the expansion causes a disturbance in equilibrium, as you have discussed. You are an accumulated vibrational component of that expansion. It is an energetic frequency composed of all the desire, the understanding or preference, and the energy that came before it.

What does this mean for your projects? I've been describing this behavior throughout the book but will relate it more directly here. Let's say you work closely with another member of your team and have been getting along well. The co-creation between you felt resilient and empowered until one day, you both felt in aggressive disagreement about a decision from management on the project you were working on together. It does not matter what this decision was at all. The result was you felt injustice in the direction and your teammate embraced it.

When the news of the change came out and you felt the angst of the injustice, you expanded right then. Your non-physical aspect of awareness just expanded to include a new awareness. This expansion changed the energy flow in the current you were experiencing. This change in flow to you felt like injustice because you had not accepted the new awareness yet. Your teammate who embraced the change did adjust to the expansion easier by not resisting the awareness and realizing it through his process into his subjective reality. With you resistant to this expansion, you block this new perspective from being realized at this moment. Again, since the energy system in your current is now increased yet you are not allowing the increased energy to be realized in you, you feel lousy. It is this lousy feeling that leads you to blame and state how much injustice has occurred and how wrong management is for their dumb policy. However, it is you not adjusting to the changing flow of energy in the universe. That is it. Your awareness has not realized the new energy that you created when you expanded. When you do you realize it, you will feel better, and when you actualize it into the objective reality, you will feel even better. If you hold it away and don't allow the new patterns to be created through the processes of realization and actualization, you will feel a struggle with the project and your teammate until you do. It's not the fault of the business or management. It is not the fault of your teammate. It is your resistance to the current awareness of the universe and your unique perspective of it. Find relief to this resistance and you will find the improved thoughts that lead you to feeling so much better and the project again moving forward expectedly.

VIBRATION-EXPANSION CONTINUUM

"If you follow the classical pattern, you are understanding the routine, the tradition, the shadow – you are not understanding yourself."

— BRUCE LEE

Everything is built on what has come before, and our conscious awareness is no different. You can't understand this present moment without the basis of what all has come before it to create your relationship. As you experience new thoughts, experiences, emotions, interactions, and coincidences, you always contrast the newness with the experience from your past.

Every concept you understand has this vibrational component too. There is a non-physical aspect of it that expanded in your awareness and vibrates from that expansion as described. You translate these vibrations without realizing it directly as thoughts, feelings, and emotions.

The physical world has the co-created space-time continuum, the objective reality, and the subjective reality. The non-physical world has the vibration-expansion continuum, the collective reality, and the vibrational reality. You exist in all of them all the time, but in your physical form, are largely aware of only the objective and subjective realities. These are just the mostly physical aspects of your world.

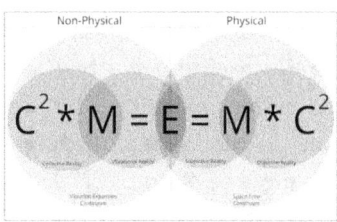

To truly get the projects and people in your life to perform well, understanding these non-physical relationships is important. In fact, the co-creation of the non-physical and the physical together is what you are as an eternally-evolving, emotionally-expressing, energetic entity. This means that the perceptions of your projects are directly related to your relationships with the energy flow of the projects.

You are always an interchangeable blend between your non-physical and physical aspects. You know that you are interchangeable because of mass and energy equivalency. You understand the tensions from your two aspects as emotion. The physical environment looks for evidence empirically, as I've stated a few times. This non-physical environment provides evidence that you understand emotionally. I will discuss the energy flow and the indicators of this flow as emotional indicators more in Chapters 8 and 9.

THE BLEND

For now, it's important to understand that you are a physical being with predominantly non-physical aspects. Both sides are present in each moment, but you do not necessarily feel this blend. It's my belief that all aspects of mass and particles have this non-physical connection through energy. You have a current non-physical aspect you are tuned to, a current physical aspect you are focused on, and both aspects have their perspective of the current moment. One experiences it with resistance, and one experiences it without resistance.

What does this mean to our projects and people? It means that you have a non-physical relationship with an aspect of the vibrational frequency of the physical concept, meaning that you have a vibrational understanding of the project and you have a vibrational understanding of the people in the projects. Our vibrational translations are always culminating to this present moment, even if you are basing them on aspects of an observation that are no longer current.

This understanding of the vibration, again, is important for your understanding of people and projects in your life, for each person and each project has culminating vibration in your experience that you translate into the current moment. You believe certain things about this project or this person, and those beliefs are translated by your understanding of that vibration that was caused by your previous expansions. This awareness is your blended awareness of the present moment. Your vibrational and subjective realities blend into a central cocreation called a point of attraction. It is this blending of your energies between these two aspects that lead to your present experience – always. If you are resistant to the flow of this energy, your two aspects will not be aligned, and you will be able to tell something isn't right from the feeling of this misalignment.

AWARENESS OF PROBLEMS AND POSSIBILITI... 81

Typically, unless you already have this awareness, you identify this feeling as something wrong with the person or project you are thinking of at the time of the feeling. You want to change these outward occurrences to feel better. You identify how this person needs to change so that you can feel better. You tell them what they need to do better, and you apply force to make them move faster or to motivate them. You try to motivate the mass to accelerate through force. In this process, you continue to focus on what you don't want. This continued focus on what you don't want continues to create large discrepancies between the non-resistant aspect of this object and your current awareness, the resistant aspect of it. This discrepancy grows, and you keep applying more pressure, hoping to change things outwardly.

Eventually, this energy discrepancy is so large that something does happen; there is a breaking point and a lot of commotion. In the end, you will feel relief, for the energy did flow. You can be aware of the energy flow much earlier; you can mold the energy flow easier, as you understand these concepts more. You can begin to deliberately start to improve how you interact and how you relate with other people and things. It just takes awareness. It's just about your relationship with yourself. Remember the end of the first chapter; does self-leadership make more sense yet?

The process of realization is the process of understanding the vibration that is created from that expanding equilibrium of awareness. As it expands and vibrates at a higher and higher frequency, you translate parts of that frequency into your experience in space-time. The more of that frequency you have translated, the more of it you have "realized" into your eternal entity's perspective, your present subjective reality. The more you focus on it from this point, the more you "actualize" this concept into the objective reality from your subjective reality. It is a beautiful, eternal, and simple process – the most beautiful. The most elegant.

The energy blend is your point of creation – your point of attraction. It is a mixture of what you desire and currently believe about that desire in any one moment. In Chapter 8, I will talk a lot more about the energy flow and how you can understand more and more about what you are creating during creation instead of in post-creation hindsight once fully actualized and manifested into the objective reality.

At this point before moving on, I want to provide a story that will help relate these concepts in more ways for you. When I was younger and in charge of more people and more aspects of the company's infrastructure, I worked a lot. These were the years I would happily put in sixteen to twenty hours day in, day out. This is years before I had a consistent meditation, appreciation, and exercise practice. Then life shifted for me, I became a single parent, and this lifestyle was difficult to maintain. I tried for a couple of years, but I know my performance, my throughput, my mentality, and my value to the firm were all lower than all previous years and not improving. Life was good for my son and me, but a struggle in so many ways.

I secretly yearned for a better way. I knew I could not keep up with this lifestyle any longer and wanted so much a more relaxed experience and to feel better around my son more often. Yet, I feared losing my generous income if I left this job, and I loved working there and all I had helped to build. I continued to push forward because, I'd rationalized, I had worked so hard for where I was; I couldn't and didn't want to stop.

Shortly after this, I was sat down and told the firm was hiring a new CIO and that I would be reporting to him. It was effectively a demotion in my perspective at the time, though the right choice for the business. I remember being

AWARENESS OF PROBLEMS AND POSSIBILITI... 83

told it was happening and feeling the sadness, anger, resentment well up inside me. I felt the injustice of it, like I had wasted my time with the firm, like my contribution was not seen or valued; I was shaken. I had been disempowered.

This moment was a moment of big expansion of my mind and awareness. My mind was in massive resistance to this new and now current awareness the universe had shifted to. My resistance to it meant I created a gap between the awareness I had related to my job, this perceived demotion, and the now-changed path of the universe. This gap is the reason I felt disempowered, not because I had been, as I would come to understand.

It took a while for me to be okay with it, and the entire time I was not, I felt lousy about it. I told narratives and stories in my head about all the things I did not like about it or the person I was now reporting too. Then one day, I "realized" how beneficial it was for me. I "realized" how this was exactly what I desired because it meant less stress and responsibility for me. I "realized" how this was the correct path to the solution to my problem with overwork, parenting, and lifestyle.

This "realization" I was having is the process I have described where the expanded energy of my awareness was received and allowed into my experience. I know it because I felt relief in it. Relief to the resistance of the movement that the current changed too when I perceived I was demoted. The more I "realized," the more I began allowing the process further and "actualizing" the benefit of the lesser position more and more. Ultimately, this decrease in position was the start, of this understanding that I am sharing with you in this book. This moment – of expansion that I hated at the time because I was highly resistant to the change in motion and did not allow the new perspective, the new thoughts, the new emotions into my subjective experience – has evolved into the amazing message contained in this book.

There is another aspect I want to illustrate about this time period. I mentioned at the beginning of that story it was at a time in my life that I was working most of the time. My son was much younger then and in daycare during the day while I worked. I would drop him off by eight most days and pick him up by six most weeknights, no daycare on weekends. My weekdays were involved waking up at seven to get ready for work, make breakfast for my son and myself, and then drive him to daycare. From there I would work until 5:30 or so when I picked him up. I worked from home often during these years to save time on commuting. He and I would have time from six to nine or so when I would get him to sleep. These years, he was young, and I stayed with him until he fell asleep, which meant I fell asleep too. When I would wake, typically an hour or two later, I would work until four or so in the morning and go back to sleep a couple more hours before waking him up. I was basically napping twice a day.

The reason I explained all that is that all that movement and action I was doing physically was powered really by my prescription of Vyvanse and a steady stream of caffeine in my favorite form of a Monster and or coffee. How is this pertinent?

All of those stimulants are forms of chemical energy which are types of kinetic energy. Kinetic energy, defined as energy which a body possesses by being in motion, is tied to the concept mass and energy equivalency from Einstein's Theory of Relativity. I was literally trying to move faster and faster so I could experience less time and accomplish more. I was doing it with chemical energy. In the chapters on motions and relations, I discussed how relief to resistance is a more effective way to go faster. Well, at this time, I was applying more and more force to my physical body trying to make it go faster, and in doing so, I remained disconnected more often from the power of my current awareness. This disconnection from this energy meant I needed more and more stimulants to keep going because of the concepts of kinetic energy and momentum.

In this state where I was not allowing the conscious energy into my experience, where I was resisting it, my thoughts and my value were at a low. I was not seeing the solutions at this point, I was not allowing the new concepts to come in, I was resistant to them outright. I was creating my reality from my beliefs that I saw and experienced, which at this time were disempowering, but I still did it.

What did this mean to my projects and people situations? I was demoted so they must not have been that good, I say jokingly, but not entirely. They were not my best because I was not powered with my highest awareness in the moment, not remotely close to it. I was not even aware of these concepts and thought my angst and frustrations were all about everybody else and my life situations. More importantly, I believed that these observations were true and just for me to be upset about. Many disempowering narratives to go along with my chemical energy forced acceleration – no wonder it went the path it did. It had to, none of that is who I wanted to be.

It took me years to understand these concepts and why, but once I understood how my conscious energy flow powers this present moment, I found stimulants less and less desirable or necessary. My relationship with my energy flow became the indicator I used to control the direction of my thoughts. Not control the thoughts, just the direction, an empowering direction or a disempowering direction. The more I chose an empowering direction, the easier choosing an empowering direction became until it was the dominant direction of my thoughts. That took a few months, but I realized one day that I had not had a disempowering thought about myself or my fellow humans all day. It is grown from there, and I will go into more detail on this conscious energy flow in Chapter 8.

Let's review the highlights from the chapter before moving on. You learned that our minds and spirits are nonphysical aspects of us. You learned that our nonphysical environment is defined by nonresistance, limitlessness, and collecting of energy. These characteristics help you understand how your thoughts and concepts expand and how you experience this expansion through translating the resulting vibrational frequency of the accumulated and culminated expansion as your present thoughts and thought streams. In the next chapter, you will begin understanding how your awareness of these vibrational translations is directly reflected by your life experience in the physical world.

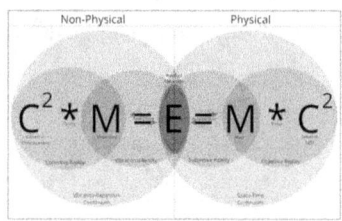

REFLECTING THE SUCCESS YOU WANT FORWARD

"Mozart's music is so pure and beautiful that I see it as a reflection of the inner beauty of the universe."

— ALBERT EINSTEIN

In this chapter, you will read about my theory of reflectivity. It is the culmination of my understanding of the previous chapters and the real reason I wanted to write this book and others. This is the chapter that I have wanted to write since I started understanding and translating these thought paths. This is exciting for me.

Let us review a little first. In Chapter 4, you learned about motion and the laws that humans agree govern motion in this universe. There are three laws that ultimately state how movement impacts physical objects. You also learned about empirical evidence through force and how momentum works. In Chapter 5, you learned about relativity and how your understanding of the world around you is relative to your perceptions and to your relationships with how fast you move and how fast what you observe is also moving. In

Chapter 6, you learned that your awareness of these observations must be a non-physical characteristic and how the mind and spirit that you have isn't part of the physical world but follows the same laws understood from the physical world. Now, in this chapter, you will learn how the non-physical and physical worlds are mirrors of each other in property and experience, and of course, why this matters to your projects and people situations – those things that led you to buy this book in the first place.

Since I started to understand that your mind's concepts of this reality in this physical world reflect your awareness in your non-physical world, I realized that this co-creation I spoke about in the past two chapters is relevant to your daily life in every way. The formula Einstein provided us for relativity is the perfect formula to reflect how you create our mental reality too. Both are forms of co-creation and can be represented as such. I believe that this formula below is a much better description of our entire reality than any that has come before it.

$$C\char`\^2 * M = E = M * C\char`\^2$$

Stated with words, the 'Current of Consciousness squared' times 'Nonphysical Movement' equals 'Energy' which equals 'Mass' times the 'Speed of Light squared.'

Have you ever noticed that a mirror would reflect anything that is cast toward it? It is non-resistant in what it casts; it is limitless in what it casts. It simply needs to collect the light directed toward it and reflect it back. The amount it reflects depends on the clarity of the optics of the mirror. You have likely seen carnival mirrors that warp you to look like an NBA center or a munchkin ready for the remake of *Wizard of Oz*. You experience your reality in a similar way as you warp the current awareness with your resistance to change. The more you cloud the reflection with resistance, the more you warp your reality toward what is not wanted. But it is 'unwanted' because you cannot see the mirror clearly, and it is the 'unwanted' part helping you define the contrast that allows you to see the clarity of the reflection.

This bulleted list below is handy as a reference for the characteristics you can understand from the reflective nature of your relationships. The first value (left side) is always the nonphysical aspect and the second value (right side) is always the physical aspect.

- Nonphysical | Physical
- Limitless | Limited
- Nonresistant | Resistant
- Collecting | Radiating
- Frequency | Force
- Frequency = Movement * Appreciation | Force = Mass * Acceleration
- Appreciation | Acceleration
- Momentum | Momentum
- Momentum = Movement * (Intention / Expectation) | Momentum = Mass * Velocity
- Nonphysical Movement | Mass
- Nonphysical Movement = Vibrance * Desire | Mass = Volume * Density
- Current of Consciousness | Speed of Light
- Expansion | Time
- Vibration | Space
- Vibration-Expansion | Space-Time
- Law of Attraction | Law of Gravity
- Expansion Dilation | Time Dilation
- Movement Energy Equivalence | Mass Energy Equivalence
- Belief Lens | Gravity Lens

- Belief Well | Gravity Well
- Conscious Energy | Kinetic Energy
- Collecting Energy | Potential Energy
- Vibration Reality | Subjective Reality
- Collective Reality | Objective Reality
- Realization | Actualization
- Point of Tuning | Point of Focus

The lookup table is an easier way to understand your nonphysical and physical relationship and the various aspects of your co-creating. As you look at the table, the characteristic derived and understood from the physical world are on the right hand, those corresponding to characteristics of our nonphysical world on the left hand.

For example, mass is defined as the product of volume and density (mass equals volume multiplied by density) physically. Both volume and density are traits of space-time. It is the volume of space and the density of the particles that are being described. This cannot exist non-physically because there isn't space-time, there is no volume, there is no density.

It did provide a clue to what the nonphysical property reflected. Nonphysical moment is the product of vibrance and desire (movement equals vibration multiplied by desire). Vibrance is the energetic quality of the expanded awareness, like volume in concept but nonphysical. Desire is the thing that awareness wants, like density in concept. Neither has physical characteristics.

Another example, acceleration is a concept that requires space-time because it is defined as the change in velocity (another physical concept meaning speed in a specific direction) over a unit of time. These concepts cannot exist non-physically but again helped me to understand the reflected concept – appreciation.

Appreciation, of course, has a couple of definitions. The first, an increase in value, and the second, a feeling of admiration, approval, and gratitude. Non-physically, both are appropriate. For a nonphysical environment has no resistance, so any attention increases value, and the pure positive energy aspect of non-physicality (nonresistant energy is purely positive) is felt as gratitude, approval, and relief to resistance.

Expansion is the nonphysical reflected quality of time. Momentum is listed on both sides because one of its definitions is a strength or force gained by motion or series of events. Our expanded awareness and translation of those vibrations are the basis of the movement that momentum non-physically strengthens. Physically, it is defined as the product of mass and velocity (momentum equals mass multiplied by velocity). Nonphysically, I have defined it as the product of nonphysical movement and intention (momentum equals movement multiplied by intention). Intention because it defines a path and trajectory or a nonphysical plan which logically is like velocity's definition of speed in a direction. I also write about momentum non-physically as the product of movement and expectation, (momentum equals movement multiplied by expectation). The reasons for this, I'll discuss more in Chapter 8. It has to do with how the conscious energies of your nonphysical intention and your physical expectation can conflict with each other, leaving your momentum as the blend, the balance between the two.

I am going to write another book deep-diving into an expanded version of this table soon. For this book, I hope this high-level understanding is a good basis for you to realize how I have come to the conclusions I have come to. I think they are simple, logical, consistent, and come with incredible implications. It is such a pleasure to share it.

NON-PHYSICAL BEHAVIORS

The physical world has a manager for mass called gravity, as I discussed briefly. All mass in the universe alters the fabric of space-time, and this alteration impacts all other mass in the universe. Gravity pulls all mass toward each other. It attracts all mass and effectively is the manager of mass in the universe. It keeps mass orderly, with structure, and predictable.

Time, as I discussed in Chapter 5, is considered the fourth dimension of our reality. Time is largely misunderstood and is always relative to the speed of the observer and the speed of the observation. Time does not exist non-physically because non-physically, there are no dimensions. Nonphysical is the "0D," or the zero dimension. This is awareness only. There are no physical constructs, just awareness that expands and builds on previous awareness as it expands.

As you learned in the previous chapter, your thoughts expand and stretch as you live your life. This expansion is the result of collecting the desire from the physical connection when a preference is created from living life. This expansion is defined by the desire and the vibrational aspect of all that came before it. It is nonphysical. You can think of it as a vibrational dot – a frequency that represents, to your awareness, that thing you think is physical in material or in concept. Your awareness of this physical thing created resistance to its change in movement; you are aware of this resistance, and you translate it as an understanding of your physical world. It is nonetheless just a vibrational frequency that you translate from the basis of all other expansions of your awareness when the translation occurs.

Non-physically, there is not gravity. Gravity requires the grid locality of space-time to be warped to be created. What you have non-physically is The Law of Attraction. Simply stated, The Law of Attraction means "whatever is liked to itself is drawn." You have common sayings in the history of our culture for this concept such as, "birds of a feather flock together," "if you lie down with dogs, you get up with fleas," and "you are known by the company you keep." In a nonphysical world of frequency, this means that all similar frequencies are attracted to each other. The Law of Attraction is the manager of all frequencies and non-physicality is limitless flow of vibrational-moving frequencies.

This formula, $C^2 * M = E = M * C^2$, says, in both a pictogram style and logical creation, that the qualitative understanding you have from relativity will apply for this non-physical environment and is another aspect of co-creation.

If energy is the product of mass and the speed of light squared, I believe that energy is defined by your accumulated understanding and awareness of those movements and is equally defined by your non-physical representation of the same thing.

The current of consciousness squared times non-physical movement equals energy, and this energy equals the current translation of resistance to this motion times the speed of light squared. If Einstein's formula is one that describes the energy that is released from destruction of mass, this formula of reflectivity is one that describes the creation of the energy that is physically understood as that mass. Awesome, right?

$C^2 * M = E = M * C^2$ is the formula of deliberate creating.

In Chapter 4, you learned that empirical evidence is evidence that you understand because of a change in force. By observing the change, you understand something occurred, and you understand that you observed something happening and now have a relationship with it. Well, in the reflected nonphysical environment, you do not understand the empirical evidence; instead, you understand this change in awareness as an energy flow, which you feel as emotion. This nonphysical aspect of us is felt, not observed, through change in force. Our nonphysical world is a world of emotional evidence, not empirical evidence. Why? Logically, because there cannot be force in the nonphysical world because the concepts of force are reliant on physical understandings. Non-physically, you have none of those things, so the same concept of higher/lower/faster/slower is one based on frequency of energy and resistance to it. The highest frequency is the current of consciousness. It is always the furthest expansion of all conscious awareness. Since it is always the furthest expansion, it is always the highest form of energy, and all non-physical movement warps this energy. Just as mass warps the physical space-time continuum, our non-physical movement warps the furthest expansion of consciousness.

The understanding of force and empirical evidence also brought that concept of momentum with it. Momentum is an important concept non-physically too, but it operates a bit differently than physically. Physically, momentum is the product of mass and velocity. Velocity is defined as the speed of something in a direction. Direction isn't possible non-physically, nor is the concept of speed. Non-physically, you do not gain speed of thought from momentum; our plan changes and our intentions clarify and the vibrational frequency you are translating from that expanded awareness increases. Intention non-physically is a nonresistant path toward the higher energy of the expanded awareness.

You will resist this intention energy with your awareness of and belief in this now and past realities objectively. They define your "belief" and "expectation" conscious energies. These energies blend with your "desire" and "intention" conscious energies at your point of attraction. It is this vibrational blend that the law of attraction responds to always. It is this balance, this blend, that you build momentum non-physically with too.

VIBRANCY AND DESIRE

Mass is defined in space-time as the product of volume and density of an object. The volume and density are both physical concepts in that they require space-time to be possible. Volume is a measure of how much space is consumed by something and density is a means of how solid that something is in our interpretation.

I've defined non-physical movement in vibrational-expansion as the product of vibrancy and desire. Vibrancy means the energetic quality – the resonance of the thing. Desire is defined by what it is that you want non-resistantly; it is defined by awareness of the contrast of what you don't want.

It is important to remember the qualities of non-physical are limitlessness, non-resistant, and collecting. This non-physical movement expands as our awareness of a preference happens from our physical experience. The non-physical side of us expands to accommodate the new energy and new concepts, while the physical side remains focused on the existing translation.

These non-physical co-creations respond to the same laws of the universe you have already discussed. The laws of motion apply to this movement and the qualitative understanding from relativity also applies.

Applying the three laws of motions to our nonphysical thought means:

1. A nonactive thought is not moving and doesn't have an active vibration in you. A thought that is in motion can only increase, since there is no

resistance non-physically; it can only get larger. Therefore, the non-physical is always expanding.
2. Force does not exist, but frequency does. Frequency is increased through appreciating the nonphysical movement or expansion. The appreciation always increases the frequency of the nonphysical movement.
3. Momentum applies to active thoughts. The more you think, the more you build up an expectation and intention of what is coming next. This expectation increases the more you think a thought. Without resistance in the non-physical world, this momentum only increases on active thoughts. Therefore, the more you think something, the more real it seems and the more you will likely think these thoughts in the future.
4. The third law stated that each force has an equal and opposite force, and each action has an equal and opposite reaction. Non-physically, it means that when you have a problem, there is a corresponding vibration of a solution. When you ask a question, there is a corresponding nonphysical movement or vibration of that answer. They are different frequencies and require different tuning to translate, but they are created simultaneously. It is up to you which you focus on most. In a project context, this means that each problem has a solution; it must, for was created simultaneously, but the focus on the vibrational expansion of the problem leaves you translating from that perspective and unable to find the expanded frequency of the solution.

Some of the understandings from relativity are interesting

when applied to non-physicality. I discussed time and expansion as reflections of each other, but what about mass and energy equivalency? Yes, non-physically, it is movement and energy equivalency, effectively what this formula now states is that there is equivalency between our non-physical awareness to movement and our physical resistance of that movement – our mass. Is it starting to make more sense how believing is seeing?

LENSES AND WELLS

The concept of the physical gravity lens reflected non-physically is a vibrational lens, or said another way, it is a belief lens. It is a lens you perceive the universe through based on the understanding of the mass and resistance to movement already in your life. As you translate a vibrational frequency, it is realized into a subjective meaning to you physically. This subjective meaning becomes your belief about what is real – what is true. It is what you understand at this time, here and now. It is what you believe to be true. The truth of it is completely limited to your understanding and your perspective of that mass and light co-creation. As you have a frequency you focus on, the Law of Attraction brings all similar frequencies toward each other, so you translate and understand this current moment from the experiences of your past, all those the things you are identifying as resistant to changes in motion. You create this reflection of your present as you hold onto these thoughts and resist the current that is flowing to you now. The current is always the expanded version of what you want and is always flowing to you. It is up to you, in the present, whether you allow this energy to flow through you or you resist it.

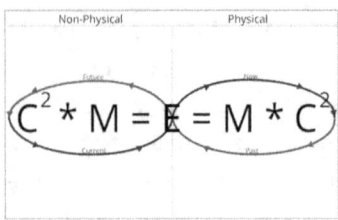

This formula and image describe the energy flow of the present. You understand the physical side of time as "now" and the "past." You acknowledge these because you experience them physically in space-time, you have empirical evidence of what is happening and what happened in the past. You have a concept of the future that has not been created yet and how this future somehow comes into our experience physically. Stated differently, you "now" flows into you "past," your awareness of the "past" creates the resistance to movement which is the contrast that defines your "future" expansion that flows in the "current," powering your "now."

A gravity well physically creates all the things that other mass orbits around through warping space-time. You might understand that well as the sun's gravity that keeps all the other planets in perfect orbit. You create this similar experience non-physically with the concept of belief well, attraction well, or vibrational wells. Those are three terms for the same thing. What these wells are is much like the gravity well. The larger and denser the mass, the larger and denser the warping of space-time created by it. Non-physically, the larger and more active the vibration, the more other vibrations impact your experience. The more you see the world through these belief wells, the more related to them you define as true. It is only true because the previous thoughts made it true to you in your perspective – that is it. At any moment, you can take these perspectives and change them to be different, molding and influencing all the changes that come after it. This is a subtle way of saying that you are defining your future through which aspects of your past you focus on.

Physically, there is a concept of kinetic energy. This, as you remember, is the energy of a body just by being in motion. Physically, there is also the concept of potential energy, which is energy that is being stored by a physical process/object until it is released. Reflectivity says there are nonphysical concepts to mirror these.

Kinetic energy is reflected to be conscious energy. Just as kinetic energy is broken down into categories of sound, heat, light, and mechanical, conscious energy is broken down into our desire, expectation, belief, and intention. Physically, potential energy is broken down to chemical, gravitational, nuclear, and elastic. Non-physically, at this time, I just call it collected energy. This is the energy that is collected and expanded as you define your desires by living your life. It is nonphysical and conscious energy; it is the collection of all our desires and wants. The well around this collection is so vast it could be called the "Well of Being," since all your being is understood from the concept of this aggregating and culminating collection of awareness and desire.

Do you realize that I've just described and supported a mechanism that states well-being is the foundation of your future, and you created this well-being for you, through you?

The co-creation of your non-physical aspects creates the continuum of vibrational-expansion. The co-creation of your physical aspects creates the continuum of space-time. The co-creation of the vibrational-expansion and space-time continuums create the eternal-entity continuum which you are central to.

Physically, you know you focus can focus because it is a

light-based experience. Non-physically, you know you can tune because it is a vibrational frequency experience.

The eternal-entity continuum is where you exist. You are the blend of both the vibrational-expansion continuum and the space-time continuum. The point of your experience in life seems to be creating a meaningful blend of these two aspects of you in this present moment, in as many present moments as you can achieve. As you live your life in the objective reality, you encounter various flows of energy and you make preferences about these energies. When you do this, your non-physical aspect expands to incorporate this newness instantly by collecting and integrating that desire into the rest of the current of consciousness. It is your job to then realize this new energy into your eternal-entity experience and bring more focus to it, actualizing it into your objective reality. The speed it is actualized is fully dependent on how much the conscious energy is aligned between your physical and nonphysical aspects. Said another way, do your desires and intentions align with your beliefs and expectations?

PROJECTS AND PEOPLE

How does this concept relate to your project and people resource? Well, every single concept you have about a mass or a resistance to change in movement in this universe has a corresponding vibrational frequency that you are aware of non-physically. The non-physical awareness of this concept is an expanded form of it compared to the physical perspective. I will discuss understanding this flow of energy more in the next chapter, but for now, you can understand that the nonphysical side is a collecting and expanding environment and has expanded to the furthest desire of what this matter means to you physically. It is expanded to the improvement that you want for it. It has – it is done. It must be done. It is Newton's third law. At the time the problem frequency is identified, the solution frequency is already created and available to be tuned to. Does this make some sense? Maybe this seems too good to be true?

If you want your projects to move faster, you need to have awareness of the problems of that project already. As you focus on those problems, they get bigger because, as you remember, there is only adding to things in your concepts mentally (non-physically); you only expand. The more you think something, the more focus is brought to it, and the more it expands. The more it expands, the more similar vibrational lenses you perceive thought through and the more vibrational belief wells you create. It's constant. It's consistent, and it's amazingly simple once understood.

The next chapter is about understanding this flow of energy and what it means to you and how you detect it. For now, understand that the nonphysical only expands and gets larger. The focus and resulting preferences you have in the physical world is what is being collected by your nonphysical aspect. It is expanding to your true wants and desires about these concepts and matters you have focused upon.

How do I know it expands?

I know it expands because it is non-resistant. As you resist the flow of energy from your physical perspective and hold onto a concept of a physical resistance to change in motion, you create resistance that then creates contrast in your present. The flow of energy from the current is always coming to you, but as you resist this flow of energy, the nonphysical aspect reflects off the resistance and increases in magnitude because it's nonresistant, is collecting momentum, and is limitless.

I love the simplicity of understanding. I love that I can represent the physical and nonphysical experience through a simple formula illustrating the co-creation of them both and their resulting co-creation.

$C^2 * M = E = M * C^2$ – the current of consciousness squared times the product of our nonphysical expansion is equal to energy which then is equal to mass times the speed of light squared – is the most beautiful and simplistic formula I can imagine providing, explaining how and what you do in this life experience. It is so easy to understand how you create your relationships and experiences in your life, in your projects, and in your relationships with people by grasping that your internal world and external world are necessary for your experience in this universe. In fact, it might be better to call your universe your "You-Inverse" because you are the center of your experience in this process and have inversed from the nonphysical awareness to a physical experience.

Your comprehension and current understanding of all that is in your life are directly related to your resistance to the moment and the newness that you've created through living your life. Projects are successful or not. People are wonderful or a challenge. In each instance, it is rarely about the person or project you are focused on; it's largely about the energy flow between your two aspects that creates your present experience.

Truly, this is an amazing experience. The more I learn, the more I understand that you are the individual creator of your individual creation, and the way you feel now is a direct representation of the way you create. The amazing part that I've learned from all this is that it is always the present. You are always in this present moment flowing energy and allowing it, or not allowing it, into our experience. You have indicators of this flow and will discuss it all in the next chapter.

Time dilation, to refresh your memory from Chapter 5, is

the concept understood from relativity that says time is relative to the observer based on the speed they are traveling. It is a bit mind-bending. I first came to this understanding from an article that talked about how photons, massless particles of light, do not experience time. When I compared expansion non-physically to time physically, I realized that it is a similar experience. In fact, it is the same experience, for the current of consciousness does not experience the expansion; it is just the expanded version. Your description of the size of the expansion is about your perspective of it from where you are now. if you describe a thought or an idea as big or massive, you are talking about the difference you observe in where you are right now in our belief and expectation and where this expanded version of our awareness is in this present moment.

Interestingly, relativity also teaches us that objects moving nearer to the speed of light are shorter in length relative to objects moving slower. Again, you describe our expansion non-physically in similar terms. You describe expansive energy you are close to as the next logical step, whereas expansive energy you are further away from, you describe as bigger, more challenging, or impossible.

ATTRACTION AND THE PRESENT

This is another interesting bit of information. The Law of Gravity keeps masses organized, as I've discussed, through gravity wells and warping space-time. The Law of Attraction keeps the vibrational expansions of the non-physical organized by keeping similar frequencies near each other.

This means that if you perceive that there is a problem with your project, no matter what that problem is, your focus on that problem is your focus toward that frequency. If you focus on that frequency – the frequency of the problem – you are unable to get to the frequency of the solution, for they are not in the vicinity of one another, they are opposites. Remember Newton's third law – equal and opposite. What the Law of Attraction would have in the vicinity of the frequency of the problem would be more problems. If the problem was identified as lack of time, for example, then what you experience is more lack of time in all you do because the vibrational frequencies near the frequency you are focused upon is that of lack and all you would be translating in that moment would appear to have more scarcity.

Therefore, in a project, when you focus upon what isn't working, you find more and more of what isn't working. When you focus upon what is working, you find more and more of what is working. Both frequencies are responding to momentum, so both frequencies get bigger when you focus on them. It's amazing, I think, and the conclusions up to now support this connection. Now that you understand this concept, why would you ever focus on what is not wanted? Well, you do it because you aren't aware of what you are doing, or you do it to create more detail from the contrast that better defines what you want and desire. That is how it works.

As you focus upon what isn't wanted and resist the flow of the current into the present, the portions you resist are reflected forward to the collection of awareness and desire, the current of consciousness. This forward-reflected energy culminates with the rest of your desires you have collected over this life and others that have not been realized yet. You physically are aware of this energy as the future, but it is presently vibrationally active, and once it is in your individual vibration, reality will be flowing toward you forevermore. You can't stop it because you have summoned and created the energy and expansion. It is done; it's just a matter of resistance when you finally allow the expansion to become realized and actualized into your now.

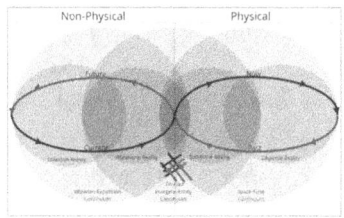

Expansion and time are the reflected versions of each other. Consider what that means. As you live life and go through time, you expand in awareness constantly, whether you realize it at this point in time or not. You live life; you make preferences in choices, creating and expanding more. The expansion flowing into the now is the current. The current powers the now with the expanded energy of your collective desires. As you experience less flow of energy from focus outside the now, generally focused on the past, you create more contrast in the now. With this additional contrast, you create more definition in the future of what it is that you desire and the vibration of it. Remember, the collection is composed of desires multiplied by vibrances, just as our space-time reality is composed of densities multiplied by volumes.

There is a trick in your awareness, and you believe that what is right now is real and true. You believe this based on the resistance to movements that you created awareness of and identified relationships with over the course of your life. It is this awareness, though, that is resistant to the change in motion caused by your expanded desires.

Let's consider what this means related to projects. As discussed in Chapter 4, there is desire to move a project faster by accelerating it. This acceleration and the results of it appear to you as a result of force, and you are gratified with empirical evidence to support the chosen direction of acceleration. Then, in Chapter 5, you learned that this evidence is relative to your motion compared to that project, including your awareness of various challenges, your awareness of various successes, the challenges in the systems, and the challenges in the industry, in the company, and in the world. You have awareness of the project as an aspect of motion related to all other aspects of motion that you are aware of. It is from this understanding, and the understanding that awareness is a non-physical trait, that you grasp how your awareness propagates to your reality – the flow of your realizations into your actualizations.

What you now are starting to understand even more is that your awareness of this aspect of space and time – your project – is reflected in your non-physical experience. The manifestation of the nonphysical is governed by inverse characteristics of the physical collecting energy, non-resistance, and limitlessness, so your physical interpretation of the project's challenges is directly related to your focus on them. If you stop focusing on what you perceive as a challenge and tune to the solutions that are also presented, you will feel much relief. It is your focus on the problem that creates the resistance, which slows down mass and warps your consciousness away from what you currently know to be.

AWARENESS OF CHANGE

How do you change this? How do you improve this behavior for your projects or your relationships? In Chapter 4, I discussed movement and also resistance to it. As you find relief to this resistance, the movement accelerates for the net force acting upon changes. Non-physically, there is not a net force. Everything is at equilibrium vibrationally. It is about frequency, so the relief you feel non-physically comes through appreciation of the vibration, the nonphysical movement you are focused upon. Physically accelerating mass causes more kinetic energy, which causes more mass, which means more and more energy is needed to accelerate an object or project faster and faster.

Non-physically, there is not resistance. Kinetic energy is not created; it is conscious energy that is created, and it's non-resistant. The more appreciation of a vibration, movement, or thought, the higher the frequency increases. Because the nonphysical and physical aspects of you are reflections of each other, you now know that this increase in frequency accelerates the physical concept of this resistance to movement. Frequency and force are equivalent but in different environments. Humans know it's impossible to speed mass up to the speed of light, and non-physically, humans can appreciate a movement until the frequency approaches the energy level at the current of consciousness. From this frequency, the power in the current is immense. Non-resisted allowing of this energy into you now results in inspiration, perfect timing, new thoughts, new ideas, new occurrences, new rendezvous, and new actions.

This is the creation of new experiences I just described and how you improve through time. You allow the culminated energy you collected to come into your now; you receive it and allow it. This is so crucial – it is allowed, not resisted. It is not fought. It is not sought after. It is not hoped for. It is not created – it is allowed. It is allowed to be. It is received. You, as the valve of the energy, allow it into your experience, or you resist it. Both are fine. You either experience the newness and improvement now or resist it and allow it to define even more contrast until you finally allow it into your experience at some other moment in your present.

No matter what, it is allowed to happen and received by you in your now.

Your focus upon the need for improvement creates resistance to improving. Your focus on the need to speed up creates resistance to the acceleration. Your focus on the wrongness of an individual for stealing a parking spot creates resistance to your energy flow as you focus on the injustice. This is where humans have the notion of unconditional love but generally fail to realize it. As I have described, it's because the creation of your desires is constantly done, culminated with the rest, and constantly flowing to you. It is only in receptive allowing that it goes through you and is not resisted. You can understand receptivity is not about the conditions, for when you are in the flow – when you are not resisting the flow of the current – you are allowing the universe to unfold at its pace, knowing that you are worthy of the goodness and wellbeing that is coming to you. You are physically a gatekeeper of this energy that you also defined. You collect your awareness non-physically and it constantly flows to you in the power of the current. If you are in a state of allowing and not a state of resistance, you allow this current to flow to you and be received through you.

Projects and people are both concepts you have awareness of physically and non-physically. As you focus upon an object or thought physically, you tune to a certain frequency of the current of consciousness that is always flowing your way. This frequency is equivalent to the force acting upon a mass physically. You can alter the force acting upon the mass to change things or you can alter the frequency you translate the vibration from and change things. Changing frequencies is always the easiest path compared to creating more force. The difference is that you feel the frequency change emotionally first. For example, your project is behind and looks like you will not make a delivery deadline. The default thought here is to force the team to work harder, do more, and overcome the obstacles that are blocking the delivery. This may work, and it may not. It is unlikely a sustainable approach regardless.

There is another aspect that might be more powerful. Find appreciation for what blocks the delivery. What does the block allow you to focus on instead? What can be appreciated by the block and the awareness of it? What does the block benefit? Why is the block blocking?

If you remember back to Chapter 4, the question words "what" and "why" can help build positive momentum. Question words "how," "where," "when," and "who" all slow it down at this point. By being more general, the questions ease resistance to the awareness. As they ease resistance, the frequency increases. You start feeling relief. As this frequency increases and relief sets in, the possibility of being able to focus on and translate the solution becomes increasingly possible. Every time. No exceptions.

As you feel the shift emotionally, your perception of the mass and your perspective of the observations about it change. With more frequency, you are at a higher level of energy, which translates physically into moving faster.

If you could have a non-resistant thought for a minute and not contradict it, you would be amazed at the physical change you would experience from this non-resistant thought with non-contended momentum. The challenge is that you have so much resistance between your two aspects. One aspect, by design, is meant to be resistant to changes in motion. It is meant, by design, to experience, export, embrace, and express from a designated orbit or a designated amount of force. The other aspect is meant to evolve instantly and provide guidance toward the evolution of the physical preferences. It is such a beautiful system – so simple, so eternal, and so perfect. So much advantage to you to understand.

The summary of this chapter is simple. If you want your projects or people to move faster, appreciate whatever aspect you are focused on instead of resisting it. The more time you spend appreciating it, the higher the frequency. The higher the frequency, the less resistance to change in motion physically. The less resistance to change in motion physically, the faster the object or concept accelerates. It is kind of a trick and yet it is not a trick at all. It is precise, deliberate, and consistent. It is based on laws as you understand them to be. It is meant to be leveraged for your advantage.

8

EMOTIONAL INDICATORS OF PROJECT SUCCESS

"I must be willing to give up what I am in order to become what I will be."

— ALBERT EINSTEIN

I love the concepts in the last chapters; they tie together well in this chapter as I discuss the flow of energy from your two aspects. Let me briefly review again. Hopefully, by this point, these reviews feel redundant. In Chapter 4, you learned about the laws of motion, force, and momentum, and you learned that there isn't just one force. In Chapter 5, you learned how everything is in motion relative to everything else, and this relative motion determines what is observed by one observer or another and how this observation co-creates relationships. Then, in Chapter 6, you learned how your awareness of what is observed – the relationship – is a non-physical characteristic of your mind, your thoughts, and your awareness. You learned the non-physical awareness is limitless, nonresistant, and collects your energetic preferences as you learn what you don't want. Then, in Chapter 7, you learned how your physical and non-physical aspects are reflected versions of each other bound through energy. And this reflection causes different behaviors in the different environments, but the concepts understood from Newton's laws and Einstein's theory fully apply and explain your conscious awareness. Finally, in this chapter, I will put it all together and talk through the flow of energy between your two aspects and how this energy flow is felt by an emotional indicator in each and every moment, if you are open to it.

If you remember the formula I shared in the last chapter ($C^2*M=E=M*C^2$), you can see that I'm stating that physical and non-physical aspects are equal and have a symmetry. I believe it's an asymmetry, as the concept of a chiral, but a symmetry, nonetheless. Chiral means that the structure and its mirror image are not superimposable – like your hands and feet. Gloves are chiral, socks are not. Shoes chiral, mittens are not. Your hands and feet are not superimposable, they are chiral. Chiral comes from the ancient Greek meaning "hand." I'm saying that your human experience has a chiral nature to it, you have a handedness about your physical and nonphysical aspects, they are mirrors of each other yet not superimposable. I believe this is also the case for anything that has mass in the physical. There is a corresponding movement in the non-physical, representing the vibration of this energetically-collected desire. I have discussed this a couple of times too, but again, as you live your life and experience contrasts in the physical, you resist the movement of the current, and in this resistance, you reflect the current back into your future. This is not the future for your non-physical aspect; it is the present. It is just the non-physical aspect of you that is not resistant to the current, so its present experience is that of your fully-expanded awareness and self.

The resistance to this expansion creates an energetic

tension between our physical and non-physical aspects, and this tension is felt as emotion. Emotions are the energy in motion between your two aspects – the physical and the non-physical. The less resistance to the energy, the more you allow into the now; the more you flow, the better you feel. The more you restrict and resist this flow of energy into your now, the worse you feel or would describe your emotional state. Since your awareness is non-physical and always expanding and always becoming more, there is not a way to decrease the energy flow on the non-physical aspect of you once expanded. It is non-resistant, it is limitless, and it is always expanding through collecting more. As you remember from Newton's first law, an object – in this case, the vibration resulting from the mind's expansion – will stay in motion until another force acts upon it. Once vibrating non-physically, it will remain vibrating since there is not a force to counter the vibration. It is always more, it is always more, it is always more. Any attention you bring to this vibration causes it to grow in strength and momentum.

This is such an important concept to understand, for you cannot push away anything. The more you try to push something away through force or through attention to it, the more you focus upon it and create it. Remember, non-physical and physical are entangled together, and the collection of energy in the non-physical is constantly flowing into our physical experience here in the present. The current experiences contrast with the past because the past is resistant to changes in motion of the current, the most resistant to changes in motion of the current. This contrast creates your point of attraction, which is the blended point the Law of Attraction responds to in your experience. Physically, it is like the center of mass for a gravity well. It is the center of your belief well.

This means that if you are out of balance between your

two sides and the energetic gap is large, the physical is at lower vibrational frequency than the nonphysical, and this lower frequency means that you attract physically a lower energy experience than what you have expanded to experience. This lower energy is felt as boredom through powerlessness depending on how much of the flow is cut off.

This energetic flow between your two sides is how you co-create individualized experiences. The point of attraction is a nonphysical aspect of you and is a blend of your conscious energies. In the physical, you build the conscious energies of belief and expectation. Belief is what you understand right now to be true from living your life. Expectation is the expected outcome based on where you are and your past experiences. Each thought and perspective that you have has a nonphysical aspect and perspective too. When you focus upon something in the physical, your non-physical has a vibration about that focus; it has a perspective that is nonresistant and a higher level of energetic vibration than the physical. It is this energetic gap that is indicated by your emotions. It is about aligning the physical and nonphysical perspectives to the most meaningful moment right here and now. The physical aspects again have conscious energies of belief and expectation. The non-physical aspect has desire and intention. Desire is nonresistant wanting – the expansion. Intention is the nonresistant plan – the paths of least resistance from where you are to what you desire.

In our point of attraction, these energies blend, and the more aligned they are, the more energy that flows into the now. You realize the vibrational energy of desire as the path of least resistance, which powers the present with inspired action that will actualize through you into your objective experience.

It works out to be represented as a grid.

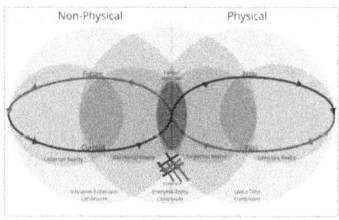

As you live your life and experience preference in what isn't wanted in your experience, you create the expanded awareness of what is wanted. Again, this is like the volume multiplied by density in the physical that is created by mass but is desire multiplied by vibrance in the non-physical movement – the expansion. The desire in the non-physical is purely high energy and always culminates with the other desires you have not yet allowed into your experience. The culmination is always flowing in the current to power your now as the form of pure intentions and paths of least resistance to get to the desired outcome. As you allow this current into your now, you experience new thoughts, emotions, inspiration, occurrences, and rendezvouses that show how your energy and perspective is changing to something different. It is the newness; it is the relief.

It is so easy to do. It is just allowing the energy instead of resisting it. Now, as that energy comes into the point of attraction, it is your belief and expectations that contrast these pure desires and intentions. The strongest force in the universe is that of non-resisted thought with momentum, but you resist these thoughts, awareness, and desires all the time and build counter momentum to them. Your current belief about what is and the current expectation about what will be are almost always in contrast with the pure desire and pure intention of your non-resistant nonphysical awareness. It is what slows manifestation, and it is what slows projects and makes you feel less than awesome. It is what leads to stress and a perspective of failure. It is so easy to change.

EMOTIONS AS INDICATORS

There have been a couple of previous authors who have written about this flow of energy that I am aware of; likely thousands more I'm not aware of. I believe my diagram of the formula explains it in the most comprehensive way that supports the results of their work. The two systems are Abraham-Hicks' Emotional Guidance Scale and David R. Hawkins' Hierarchy of Levels of Human Consciousness.

For this comparison, I am using the emotional guidance scale. For me, it is the most logical and direct way of understanding my alignment with my energy flow between my physical and nonphysical aspects. Remember from Chapter 5 that everything is about relationships and emotions are the relationship between your non-resistant expanded awareness and your resistant present perspective and focus – that's it. Embrace them for their pure beauty and power.

The emotional guidance scale states that our emotions represent our highest vibrational frequency or energy flow down through our lowest. Meaning joy, appreciation, empowerment, freedom, and love are all the highest vibrational energy you can feel. When you feel these emotions, you are nonresistant to our point of focus. When you feel fear, grief, depression, despair, and powerlessness, your focus and thought process right then are most resistant to the expanded energy flow.

That scale follows:

Joy/Appreciation/Empowered/Freedom/Love
Passion
Enthusiasm/Eagerness/Happiness
Positive Expectation/Belief
Optimism
Hopefulness
Contentment
— midline between feelings described as positive and those described as negative —
Boredom
Pessimism
Frustration/Irritation/Impatience
Overwhelming
Disappointment
Doubt
Worry
Blame
Discouragement
Anger
Revenge
Hatred/Rage
Jealousy
Insecurity/Guilt/Unworthiness
Fear/Grief/Depression/Despair/Powerlessness

The higher your energy flow, the less resistant you are to the flow and the higher on this scale you would emotionally feel when focusing and thinking a thought. The lower you go on the scale means the more you feel resistance to the energy flow of the non-physical guidance that is constantly available in your current moment as a path of least resistance to a thought that feels better.

I want to relate this back to relativity briefly before I continue. Relativity states that the highest speed possible is that of light. Mass resists this speed and therefore travels at a lesser speed. If the energy does not increase, the greater the mass, the further from the speed of light the object slows. In this slowing, more and more time is experienced -- this is the concept of time dilation again. With this guidance scale, the highest energy corresponds to a nonresistant state which is an asymmetric reflection of the highest speed a massless particle can move. With these concepts together, the emotional indicator scale also states the less resistant you are, the less time you will experience relative to any observer on a more resistant end of the scale.

Since this is about emotional guidance and indicators, I need to share from what I have experienced myself. I used an example in a previous chapter about my first perceived demotion and how I expanded in that moment. I think before the meeting, I was around the hopeful level on this scale. After being told I had to report to somebody else, the ensuing mental narration of disempowering stories quickly built momentum until I was depressed and powerless. It does not take long if you do not understand these concepts or that you have a choice in the direction your thoughts flow. I did not at the time, and soon I was all sorts of down. The momentum of that thought path was fast.

My reason for bringing it back to this experience is because I remember being in this emotional place and trying to work effectively. I couldn't work differently, not really, I thought at the time. I was operating too slowly for how fast the rest of the world seemed to operate. I had a difficult time keeping up in conversations because I felt they moved so quickly. The conversations were not any different than a few days prior to when I was not so sad. Yet in that sadness, holy cow. People and events were on fast forward. Of course, at the time this meant I wanted to take more stimulants to try and keep up which lead to less sleep and even lower energy and no replenishing anywhere to be found. Being as transparent as possible, it took years for me to work back up the scale to a consistently less resistant place.

During these challenging years, I can remember saying to a number of different people through a number of different conversations that time was speeding up. Those were my exact words, "Time is speeding up." It's only now as I write this book that I've realized the profound truth of them. Time dilation describes this mechanism precisely. Of course, it was me that was slowing down more. The objective reality's rate of time wasn't changing. My perceptions of it changed because I was slowing down. Even as I tried to correct this slowing through chemical stimulants – I couldn't reach the same speed the objective reality moved and changed. I had blocked so much energy from my reality through my focus in life that the drag could only continue to increase momentum toward what I didn't want. That being more drag, more confusion, more sadness.

It got better, of course. Looking back, the one thing that made a difference and allowed the changes and replenishment to begin for me was developing a consistent meditation practice. I'll talk about that in Chapter 10; it is the easiest tool all humans have access too. It's the one tool that allowed my reality to shift from being disempowered to empowered.

The influence you have over your perspective of focus and directions of thought flow is the way you create your experience, it's the moment you are living and all that you are defining and building right now. Often, before I understood these concepts with the clarity I now have, I did not value this real constant creating process, which led to several results I've shared with just that one story.

You now understand that you constantly have a flow of energy moving toward you and trying to move through you – a current of energy – and this flow of energy is the culmination of your wants and desires over your awareness's lifetime. You can allow this energy into your experience, or you can resist it. If you resist it, you drop further down the emotional guidance scale. The energetic gap grows larger, and if you receive the energy and allow it without resistance, you go further up the emotional guidance scale and close some of the gap.

What is so wonderful is this is an up-to-the-moment indicator that every single being has for its own life path and only its life path. You cannot vibrate for another's point of attraction even if you really, really, really, really want to. You cannot understand another emotional response to anything, not really. It is about the individual energy flow, the individual perspective, and their ability to allow this energy into their experience or to resist it. It is about your focus and perspective and your ability to receive and allow or resist and block the energy flow.

BACK TO PROJECTS

This, of course, works with your projects too. When you discuss aspects of the project, you feel certain ways. These feelings are always indicators of the energy flow, perspective, and alignment between your non-physical and your physical self. It's the same with people, as I've illustrated through my story. You fixate on how various people behave, and this makes you feel a certain way, and you blame them for how you feel. In my case, in the story I shared, it was easy to pass blame to others.

I learned it is never about the other person; it's never about the project. Instead, it is always about your internal allowing of the awareness of what the project or person is in your non-resistant expansion, blended with the beliefs and expectations at this moment. This is the resistance you have regarding this person or project. You feel it in the moment. If anything, your one job in this universe is to be aware of this feeling and to work on keeping alignment between your two aspects so you can continue to flow positive energy into your experience. Why do I believe that is the one job you and I and all awareness has in this experience? It is because this is the point of control for what is experienced individually. It is the only point of control you have. You have control over the direction of your thoughts, and therefore you have control over your vibration, and therefore your point of attraction.

If you think about the process and flow of energy a little more, I'm saying that you create the desire from your understanding of what isn't wanted, and this desire is mixed and evolved with all previous desires in the current awareness of all and this flows to you constantly. As you focus physically and have thoughts about that point of focus, you non-physically have a perspective too. This non-physical perspective is of course nonresistant and always further expanded than where you are physically. You feel physically in doubt, worried, or full of blame toward something or somebody. This focus makes you want this person to behave differently so you do not feel this way, you feel better. You blame them for it; you get angry for control and tell the other person to change or shut up. This is all about your perspective of that person based on your flow of energy. It is based on the frequency of this energy stream you are currently translating from. It is never about the person, the project, or the perceived source of this angst. It is always about your relationship between your physical and nonphysical selves and how you allow this energy to flow or not.

What is extra-amazing is that, once you start to understand how this flow of energy works, you can get to a place where you know that, in each moment, you create or recreate your experience. You are not bound to perceive the project as failing or the teammates as pathetic and inept. It is a choice always. And your choice impacts your experience the most.

That flow of energy and thought process doesn't feel good, so what does this mean? What does it indicate? What choice about your perspective and focus does it mean?

This means there is an expanded and improved perspective waiting for you to allow into your experience. It's up to you and never up to the external condition. This is a trick of your experience in this work up until now. Think about how much of the world close to you or across the earth you try to define and control how it comes about, saying what is right and wrong. You try to control people's desire to worship, their sexual preferences, how to dress appropriately, how to talk to others, what noise is, what music is, how to spend money, etcetera. Every single one of these aspects that you focus on and want to control likely makes you feel doubt or worry about it in relation to you. It's not about the thing you are focused upon; it's always about your perspective of it relative to your nonphysical, nonresistant, expanded awareness of it.

In fact, I could even go so far as to say the emotional indicators you have are because of the relationships you have with all things, but specifically it's about the relationship between your physical and non-physical selves.

There is another aspect of this energy flow that's interesting. The common term for us and what I consider myself is a "human being." What are you "being?" You are being interchangeable between the physical and non-physical aspects. Just as energy and mass are equivalent but in different states of manifestation, our nonphysical energy and physical energy are equivalent but in different states of manifestation too. The zeroth law of thermodynamics states that if $A=B$, and $B=C$, then $A=C$. Using this same logic, the term "human being" as a description allows the following wordplay. Being means existing. Existing means to be current. Thus, by the zeroth law of thermodynamics, "human being" can also be logically referred to as "human currents." I think this is equally as profound a description as human beings and equally accurate given what I've described thus far in the book.

You experience emotional indicators as your direct way to live your life the way you want. It's your current. Over time, you find that you are less sensitive to the emotional shifts that happen as your energy and perspective shift. You grow accustomed to feeling lousy, worrying, or feeling doubt or discouraged. The longer you hold onto these perspectives, the more energy is collected non-physically for what you want, and the gap in energy flow grows larger and larger, leading the emotional state to degrade more and more until you feel powerless. This is a state literally of cutting yourself off from the flow of power in the current. Your current. The current never stops flowing; the current never stops offering you the path of least resistance to a better feeling thought – never. It is always a physical aspect choice that blocks and resists this flow of current.

How can I be certain? I can be certain because it is about resistance. I have described why it is about resistance for the past four chapters from various angles. The physical aspect resists the flow while the nonphysical can't resist it because the entire nonphysical environment is nonresistant. Even if you aren't emotionally sensitive to your energetic flow, you can still identify how you feel about various observations based on the chronic stories you tell. The next chapter will discuss how these stories and narratives give you key indicators of how you are feeling and where your awareness has expanded.

ANOTHER PERSPECTIVE

I want to talk through this flow more to understand what is occurring. It is wonderful and simple to comprehend. Your physical side is mass and resistance to change in motion. It is radiating energy. It radiates, it emits, and it broadcasts energy outward. Your nonphysical again is collecting – culminating this energy. As you live life, you make choices of preference, generally without even realizing it, and this preference is reflected forward into this collection of energy. This collection of energy is, again, a non-physical concept. It is a vibration – a vibration caused by the expansion of your awareness. This vibration represents a desire and the culmination of the energy leading up to it, effectively the desire's starting point. It is constantly flowing to you. It is a flow of energy that is created for you, by you, and flows to you and through you. This is the gift of your present moment. Every moment.

You are always in this current, finding awareness to the resistance of the flow. This resistance is the holding onto of a concept's energy from the conscious aspects of belief and expectation, while the desire and non-resistant expanded vibration flows into the now as a path of least resistance. This path will take you where you want to be from where you are presently, always. It is this path of least resistance that people resist in the flow. Just as the orbits of your mass happen in paths of least resistance, the expansion of your awareness into the now happens in paths of least resistance. That is a path from the lower frequency of resistance to the nonresistant frequency in the current of consciousness.

The current of consciousness that flows to you and through you is always the furthest expanded version of that which you have become vibrationally and is translated in the present by your awareness of the contrasting resistance of movement in the physical. It is your job to realize the frequency that you are translating from.

Is it a high frequency or is it a low frequency? How do you feel? If you feel satisfied and better according to the emotional guidance scale, you're in a non-resistant frequency. This means you are powered at this moment with your focus in a way that is allowing the flow of energy into your experience. You aren't restricting it, you aren't resisting it, and you aren't pinching off the flow. Interestingly, it is this satisfied state that you naturally return to as you release resistance when sleeping or meditating. It is this state of satisfaction where you start the non-resistant momentum toward the higher vibrational feelings joy, love, appreciation, and empowerment. Isn't it interesting that there is a term called "empowerment?" This is a state of being when you are powered. It is at the top of the emotional guidance scale. At the bottom of the scale is a state of powerlessness – being completely cut off from the flow. It is beautiful in simplicity once you understand and allow your worthiness of this energy flow. In the following picture, you can see how your emotional indicators are incorporated into our co-created experience. Your awareness of the contrast between your two aspects defines how much energy you allow into the physical now and thus provides your emotional indicator for your energy flow.

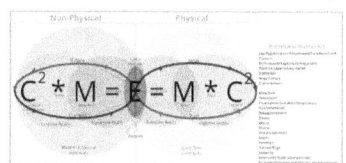

Momentum is important. Remember, the nonphysical aspect of you doesn't have friction to slow something down; it's limitless and non-resistant, so the more you focus on anything, the more of it you create. The more of it you create, the more you will focus upon it, and the more you focus upon it, the more you will create. This is logical in the physical world, but it's also logical in the nonphysical response. The nonphysical aspects of expansion, dilation, attraction, and belief lenses and wells help explain it further. Again, only being additive, the more a thought is thought, the more the vibration is made active in the point of attraction, and the more the vibration grows.

As the vibration grows larger, it impacts more vibrations in its vicinity; this is the attraction/belief well concept that mirrors the physical gravity well. The more you see the world through these wells, the more you believe these wells are the truth of the universe and the truth of your reality. They are just vibrations that you continue to activate in this present moment with your attention to them and their relationships. You can change this; you just need to be aware that it is possible and be aware of the mechanism that keeps you seemingly needing to think certain thought patterns or beliefs. They are vibrationally-created wells and lenses that continue to be activated and increased in this present moment.

This is how conscious energy works, but you are simultaneously creating the physical world and consciously creating the nonphysical expanded world. The two are literally happening at this same moment, but your resistance to the flow of energy and belief that you are in this chunk of space-time perspective keeps you from understanding your true vibrational characteristics. You can feel this, though. This is your indicator of being on your path or off your path. Your emotions are key.

For example, you have a deadline for writing a report to give to the business. You didn't want to write the report, you think it's stupid and a waste of time and believe nobody will read it, still you are required to do it by your manager. The focus on the stupidity keeps you from realizing the conscious energy flowing to you from this future self where the report is already completed. The narrative about the stupidity of the report is an indicator that the energy is not flowing as you focus that way. The focus on the stupidity and injustice of writing is your resistance to the ease of completing the report, by flowing the energy and awareness that you have already defined and collected non-physically. Through relaxing, receiving, and allowing this pre-sent and defined energy to move, the report will not be a drag to write but will be another way outlet for you to flow of your creative source. Doing this always feels incredible.

DIFFERENCE BETWEEN THINKING AND FEELING

There is a difference between thinking a thought – about how it feels to love, for example – and feeling inside yourself what it feels like to love. There is a difference between thinking and feeling. Often, you need to stop thinking, feel more, and allow the occurrences to flow to you.

An important aspect to understand in this concept is that your thoughts are translations from this energy stream based on your experience of contrast up to this moment. This translation is based on a frequency that you feel. The higher the frequency, the less resistance and the more powerful the thought is at this moment. However, the thought like this does not seem large; it seems like the next logical step because you are up to speed with the current of that stream. If you were not up to speed with it, the thought would feel huge and massive – maybe impossible. This, again, can be represented by our understanding of relativity and the concepts of time dilation and length warping at various levels of resistance.

The goal of any person on a team is to try to bring as much of this energy to their moment as they can. This means not having conflicting conscious energy in your point of attraction in that moment. Remember that conscious energy is made up of desire, intention, belief, and expectation. The desire is always the non-resistant version from your experience, it is the wanting. It flows to you with paths of least resistance as long as you aren't in opposition with conflicting beliefs or expectations. If you are focused on the present physical world and believe that to be true, the desire is unlikely to find enough solidification to manifest as desire in the physical world. Remember, the process of realization is the process you go through non-physically as you translate various vibrations into your subjective reality. The process of actualization is the next step, as the realized vibrations are solidified into the objective reality, generally through actions and impulses. This can happen quickly if those conscious energies are aligned, or it can never happen until the entity kicks the bucket and releases all resistance at that moment. What I am explaining is that the desire happened at expansion; it's been created and it is the solution to the problem, the answer to the question, the giving to the asking, the opposite action in Newton's third law – it's done. You just need to figure out how to release the current focus and allow the new higher energy frequency thoughts to flow into your experience.

The answer to going faster is in releasing resistance. Non-physically, this releasing of resistance can happen through appreciation of the vibration (the concept, the experience, the observation). It is in appreciating that you increase the frequency. As the frequency increases non-physically, it is constantly increasing in power. If you follow Hawkins' research on this conscious energy, you will understand that it's a logarithmic scale, meaning the upper and lower bounds are magnitudes different in energy but represented within the similar distance on a graph or the chart I provided. The power of nonresistant thought is so immense compared to anything that is resisted.

The power to improve the team's performance and overcome obstacles is so present within you right now. It is a matter of releasing resistance to the improved version, the improved thought, or the solution's vibration, instead of holding onto the resistance of what is. It is possible to do that right now. It is possible to release the resistance right now. Although, if you've been thinking the other way for some time, and I assume you have, there is a substantial amount of momentum built up that resists that instant change.

This momentum makes it seem like you can't change, but you can. You just need to understand that vibration is always additive, so you can't stop thinking a thought that is active with a lot of momentum in you. You need to change the topic, change the focus, and change the vibration that is active to anything else that feels better.

To stop thinking a thought, you replace it with another concept. You find a different aspect to focus on. In doing this, you can release resistance, and in doing that, you will get to a higher frequency of thought.

In a previous example, I described a looming deadline for a report that was forced upon you. As you focus on the injustice of the request, you block yourself from the higher frequency vibrations. To find relief to this thought path, you can focus on literally anything that feels better, it does not have to be work or report related. Anything at all that feels better, and as you begin to feel better, you can turn your attention back to the report from a now-higher frequency of thought.

It is from these higher frequencies that you will be able to tune to the solution or completed report and allow it to be received through you. It is received through the process of realization to be actualized objectively through the process of actualization.

This is often when taking a walk or getting up and staring out the window helps when you have been stuck or find yourself frustrated. It is because of your focus shifts from something highly resistant to something without resistance. From this higher frequency of thought, if you turn your attention back to the thing that is troubling you with the high momentum, this higher frequency will have a different perspective and will alter that unwanted vibrational momentum to start changing it to a new direction. As the old momentum catches back up to you, you will feel less than satisfied again; it is time to change this thought again and focus on something else. Work your way back up the emotional scale, and once stable at a higher non-resistance frequency, you can turn your attention back to the issue bothering you. In this way, you improve the old stories or awareness and do not create more of what is not wanted. It is a subtle dance, a game to be played, but once you understand how this flow works and how you are creating, you will understand it more and more. It will be easier and easier. Your projects, people and life in general will feel noticeably improved and more fun than ever before.

EMPOWERING YOUR SUCCESS OR FAILURE STORIES

"Follow your bliss and the universe will open doors for you where there were only walls."

— JOSEPH CAMPBELL

I'm so glad you are still reading. With a basis of understanding you started in Chapter 4 and built upon, you now have a powerful platform to detect and change the stories or narratives you chronically tell yourself. Why do you want to change this chronic narrative? I could probably write a few pages just with reasons you want to change this narrative. They would be my reasons, not yours and thus, mean less to you. It is important to find your reasons, those things that matter most to you. A few suggestions are to improve the quality of your life, to influence projects success, to improve the velocity of your projects, to improve the relationships with the people you cross paths with, and to embrace the energy you created for yourself that wants to flow to you and through you in every moment of every day.

That last one is mine and when you become aware of this energy flow, you will want to feel it often too.

A small recap for what you learned up to now, which should be redundant at this point, nonetheless these are new concepts and the repetition helps build momentum. Chapter 4 described the laws of motion in this universe. You read about inertial, force, and physical momentum. In Chapter 5, you studied that this motion is observable and the observation itself depends on the perspective – the relationship between the observer (you) and the observed. In Chapter 6, you realized, through reading, that this observation is your awareness; it's your conscious awareness. I then shared that this conscious awareness is, at the simplest form, awareness of a preference and resulting expansion of energy flow, and all this universe has grown from the collecting and evolving of the awareness of movement, of this choice in flow. Each movement is self-aware. Each movement is conscious of itself in the same way you are conscious of yourself, just on a different scale. This awareness grows from the most simplistic to the most complex, as the movement or the vibrations culminate into more and more.

In Chapter 7, I discussed my theory that the universe reflects our physical and nonphysical selves, and this reflection honors the laws of the universe within different environments – the physical and the non-physical. Finally, in the previous chapter, you discovered that these two aspects of you flow energy continually back and forth, creating evolving contrast to be experienced in the present while you emotionally experience this flow of energy as an indicator, as your guidance, to what you want and what is collected and defined in your future.

This is the most simplistic and beautiful system I could imagine. I think it is ideal to get to live a life that is molded to what I want by living it and detecting the slowing of energy – the resistance to energy that creates the newness that I want – the non-resisted energy to enhance my life as I'm willing to receive and allow it to. This is exactly what I have described thus far in this book. This is exactly what is happening. I'm describing how these mechanisms influence projects and people in work environments. Obviously, the contexts can be changed but the core interactions I described continue to apply.

Along the way, I discussed various aspects of how this energy, this flow, and these laws can impact the narratives you tell about the projects and people you have in your experience. How often is the tone of your conversation about a project described or felt as positive? How often do you praise the project and all that is growing from it compared to how often you complain or focus upon an aspect of the project that is not working? How often do you come up with a pros and cons list and debate it heavily before moving forward with a project? All these questions are great, I will examine this last question and play with it some to bring more awareness to the process with energy and focused added.

Knowing what you now know about the laws of the universe as I've described them to be and about the flow of what is wanted and the resistance to what isn't wanted – how do pros and cons lists influence this movement? Do they build up desire? Do they create clarity of the conscious energy that is in your point of attraction? Remember, this conscious energy in your point of attraction is the blending of your physical and nonphysical at this moment. It's the aspect of you that The Law of Attraction is attracting to. It is the blend of conscious energies that are defined by what is wanted (desire), what is planned (intention), what is believed to be true (belief), and what is the expected outcome (expectation). You further should ask what is the frequency you are vibrating at? What is the emotion you feel as you go through a pros and cons list?

Likely, you don't feel anything because you are so used to this process and so used to feeling indifferent about it. This feeling is an indicator of energy flow. It is subtle, but the way you discuss your projects chronically or think about them indicates this flow of energy and whether you allow it or not.

What happens if you don't allow it? For starters, you become more resistant to the conscious energy that it represents. Said a different way, the beliefs and expectations you have are contrary to your nonresistant desire and the intentions being offered to you as paths of least resistance. As you resist more, you create more of the improvement and the gap between your two aspects increases. You build the momentum of belief and expectation conscious energies for your validating focus. Each moment forward validates why you should believe and expect what you are experiencing. This leaves you feeling worse and worse as the energy tension between you starts to indicate that there is a problem, and you start feeling worried, blameful, insecure, or worse. Most of the time, this state of worry is translated into a problem with the project. It is an aspect of the project that you are focused on and do not feel is working out well or think is moving too slowly. This is likely a completely accurate observation and completely valid.

The question is – is this an observation that you want to take into your next expansion as you create your life, or is it one that you can find a better perspective of and take that improved perspective into the next expansions and start the process of feeling better about it?

Both choices are valid, but only one will flow more energy into your now. It is the flow of energy in the now that allows the improvements to occur. The flow of energy comes in the form of thoughts that feel like relief when you think of them in context of the project. They will feel like inspiration if you aren't near their energy, if there is a large gap. The larger the gap, the larger the inspiration feels. This means this conscious energy might feel huge, like a mission statement or something grandiose, as you briefly experience the clarity that is possible when you don't create a contradiction to the desire -- the desire that was created and answered when you had the question initially.

Remember, Newton's third law of motion stated that there isn't just one force and each force creates an opposite equally. This is the trick that is most useful in the project world. How to experience the contrast of the project's pain long enough to create the improvement in the collected energy of your nonphysical awareness and allow it to power your now with new perspectives, thoughts, and emotions quicker. This is the secret to accelerating projects and people. It is learning the art and the dance, between creating the contrast and immediately refocusing from the problem to the solution that is created in the contrast.

There is an old saying about turning the other cheek to avoid a fight. I think it describes turning focus away from what is unwanted and turning it toward what is wanted. This is the subtle nature of the universe, since you always create more of what is focused upon in that moment. The focus on what is wanted will allow that change in your life experience far faster than focusing continually on the aspects of the now that are unwanted even if "true."

THE PERSON DIFFERENCE

Is this the same with the people in your life – the coworkers and teammates who are working well or aren't? Yes, of course it's the same concept. The difference with people is that they are more dynamic than projects. They have personalities and abilities to focus on what is wanted and unwanted. They all have points of attraction, and this point of attraction is not something that you can change. You cannot vibrate for another; you cannot feel for another. You can never truly understand the emotions of another, and you can never truly understand the motivation or desires of another. They are theirs and theirs alone. They are your and yours alone.

This is the true beauty of the universe. We are all having this experience and we are all the center of our own universe since we all inversed from this nonphysical awareness. This creation of your universe – your unique aspect of it – is for you to manage and you to own. The more you give this power to others, the less you feel positive about it. It is a common thing to do because people seem to be taught early in most life experiences not to feel worthy of their desires or their wants. Often, they do not feel worthy of even having a life that is happy, fulfilled, and abundant. People feel as if they need to suffer so they can be worthy later when they are dead. They feel that if they are not working hard, the results will not be worth it, and they feel that without massive sacrifice, no gain or improvement is possible. "No pain, no gain" is truly a statement of ignorance and naivety of this flow of energy.

Buddha said that pain was required when living this life, but suffering was optional. This is basically what I have described in choosing your points of focus. You can focus on the pain or you can focus on the improvement; either way, it is your choice. It is only your choice. This is the best gift ever – your present.

The only thing you can control is your focus and how you feel about what you are focused upon. This control of focus and thought is the first level of manifestation or actualization from the nonphysical to the physical. It is the feeling you desire, you just think that it's about the big manifestation that matters, it's about completing the project that matters, or it's about moving your people faster that matters. Again, these are all forms of empirical evidence of the force you applied to change the world around you, and hopefully you feel better because of it.

It is not the only way to experience evidence.

What I've described is a way to feel the evidence and feel the improvement along the entire path toward the manifestation of the completed project. In fact, each improved thought you create from the realization through actualization process is a manifestation, they are the treasures along the journey, and they are abundant. Each is a present wrapped just for you waiting to be unwrapped only by you.

It is about the process, and the process is the reward. This is the process of you realizing that you do not like a thought; realizing that you can change it is rewarded with the improved energy. This is the process of realizing an old story you tell about somebody or something that is not serving you anymore, changing it to a better one, and feeling better about it. That is the reward. The rewards come to you and are manifested immediately as the energy in the current flows and powers your now. This is the description of why people say, "the joy is in the journey, not the destination." It is the same concept. Find the love and flow at this moment and in all moments you can, it makes the most difference to you.

Why do you want to find this higher frequency and not resist? I tried to describe this behavior in the previous chapter on energy flow. It is about the frequency of the energy you allow in your current moment that matters to you most. As you are resistant to the current of energy, you have the same result that mass does to the speed of light. It slows it down, it warps it, it increases your experience of time, and the world seems to go faster while you appear to go slower.

Really, you want the opposite. You want the world to go slower while you go faster; it's an advantage. How many superhero stories are about having superspeed? How many are about having super slowness? I googled this from curiosity. The slowest superhero, according to Google, is named Whizzer. He debuted in 1941 and could run 100 miles per hour. That is the slowest superhero, 100 miles per hour. Super slowness is the suckiest of all superpowers, apparently.

You want the projects and business problems to slow down so you can deliver faster. Remember the concept of time dilation from relativity? This is exactly what happens as you slow your thoughts down and resist the flow of energy. I experienced and shared how this worked for me when I was sad and down at specific times. The gap in your energetic areas between what has been collected and what you are allowing gets larger. This gap resists more energy flowing through you in the present and this resistance makes you feel slower, just as you know mass slows down more and more as it increases and resists more.

It is such a cool understanding to grasp this. Just sit with it for a moment and understand that you experience this for a reason; it's so you can calibrate yourself to what you want. As you appreciate this energy to close the gap, the frequency of the energy you translate from increases. This higher frequency allows new perspectives and thoughts as it is allowed into the physical now. It is a higher-speed thought – a more powerful thought-form. It is where the solutions to problems will be found. It is where the inspiration comes from to leap past where you are in the project, and it answers so many blocks. It is where you will find the success you want. It must be there; it is law, right? This is not made up, you live life with these laws, and you use them or are abused by them. I love it. I think it is glorious that you get this level of decision-making and empowerment.

In previous chapters, I've shown the co-creation of our aspects. The formula I shared ($C^2 \ast M = E = M \ast C^2$) is perfect for understanding our co-creative aspects of this life experience. It can be read as a sentence that describes our experience.

If you think of this in a different way, it might be easier to see. The current of consciousness is collecting and integrating desires as they happen through living life. This current is a collection. You would understand it as a spiral, since it is always getting larger. *Phi* is likely a good representation of it. Phi is termed the Golden Ratio and experienced through nature seemingly everywhere you look. It can be described through the Fibonacci sequence which stated most simply as a sequence of numbers where each new number is the sum of the two before it. For example, zero, one, one, two, three, five, eight, thirteen… An example of Phi is often provided by the spirals of a seashell, but it's prevalent throughout nature from the ratios in the human body to the structure of flowers. Physically, you radiate energy, and this is in the form of a wave. The collection is a spiral and the expression is a wave. The wave and the spiral are the same thing but from different perspectives. How incredible is that?

Non-physically, you can tune to a frequency like a radio. This is because it is all vibration in awareness. Everything is a frequency of nonphysical movement or expansion. Freedom, joy, love, depression, money, poverty, brilliance, and kindness are all frequencies. All concepts and matters have a frequency. Your understanding of physical aspects is a complex mix of these frequencies in your point of attraction. The more aligned you are between your conscious energy flows (desire, intention, expectation, and belief), the better you feel this moment. In the formula, you see this described perfectly. The asterisk (*) symbolizing multiplication also symbolizes that you tune nonphysical to the frequencies in the current of consciousness and you focus on your perspective of light and mass. These two aspects either are compatible or they aren't. When they aren't, you don't feel so good and when they are, you feel good.

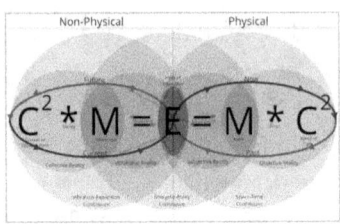

This is the same concept you have when you look at an aspect of a coworker or a project. You feel a certain way, and this feeling is based on your energy flow. This energy flow is based on what you believe and expect physically from the history of living life, the preferences you made, and what you created as improvements vibrationally.

FOCUS MATTERS

"That the soft overcomes the hard, and the yielding overcomes the resistant, is a fact known by all, but practiced by few."

— LAO TSE

You are focused on Bob not delivering his part of a project from the previous three deliveries. The narrative that begins to build in you and other teammates is that Bob cannot deliver, that Bob is the reason the team will not succeed, and that Bob is going to cause you to fail.

In this focus, you feel bad and you think the project's probability of failure is because of Bob's actions, but it is not.

You feel bad because you are focused on the aspects of Bob that have cut you off from your flow of energy – that's it. By cutting off the flow of energy, you are blocking the new thoughts that will help you understand that Bob's challenges are for a reason. The faster you can appreciate the issues and contrast he creates, the faster you will feel relief on the delivery you are focused upon. It is your focus on the lack of his delivery that causes your disharmony with yourself and your energy flow. It is never, ever about the external circumstance. Your emotions and thoughts are always about your present vibrational frequency and what that means you are resisting or allowing. Your desire to change Bob so you can feel better is also an approach that will progressively feel worse. There is a path to overcome this; there is a way to appreciate Bob's work even when it appears that he isn't doing good work at all.

You see, The Law of Attraction is responsible for all the frequencies that you attract in your point of attraction. These frequencies are based on what you are focused upon. The focus upon Bob's lack of good work is you focusing in opposition to the improved version of Bob's work you created in your future collection of desires. It is there – it must be. It is a law of the universe. It is already done, you just need to find relief to your present focus and allow the improvement in.

You see, as you focus on the lack of Bob, the only thing Bob can possibly deliver to you are lacking experiences because you are focused on Bob's lack. That's mind-bending, isn't it? Still, everything in this book up to this point has been explaining this concept. You are responsible for the experiences in your life based on the mix of vibrations in your present point of attraction. The point of attraction is always what The Law of Attraction is basing its management of frequencies around for you. Focusing on Bob not being amazing creates a vibration that means Bob cannot be amazing in your experience, even though he may totally want to be amazing. You see, it is your awareness – your relative relationship with Bob – that creates your experience at this moment.

With this awareness, what is a better story you can tell about Bob? It is easy. Just make it generally believable to yourself so you do not create more resistance to this new story. "Bob is a great worker; he's improved since he started. He does not always deliver, but he is meticulous, and you know the work he does deliver on is always great quality. Bob is a smart and a diligent worker. He understands the company's needs and the planned roadmap. I enjoy working with Bob most of the time. I know he is doing his best, and sometimes things come up, but I know he is doing his best to meet these objectives. I know Bob is learning and growing too. I know I can help him find relief to his resistance, and I can help him prioritize his flow a little better. I know Bob wants this project to succeed. I know Bob wants me to succeed as his manager. I also know that Bob can do the work, he is perfect for the task, and he is getting better all the time. I know that, even if Bob does not turn it around this week, he is improving and it's getting better all the time. I know that I can help Bob find his power and can help him allow his greatness to flow forth. I know it is possible because I'm starting to understand this flow in me more and see the results in my experience. I know Bob can do it, I know he will do it, and I know he *is* doing it. I appreciate the efforts Bob is making. Even when I do not see it, I know Bob is trying and doing the work. In time, I know you will get things running well, and Bob's momentum of success will be immense. I know this is going to be a great project, and I know that Bob is a great teammate. He is a snappy dresser and he is fun and funny. I like working with Bob. He's a great guy."

Now, none of this might be true, or it all might be true. The point is that you want to find a story that does not create negative momentum or isn't counter to the conscious energy you've created in your current of awareness. When I first started hiring people and delegating the many hats I wore, I learned this lesson intimately.

I was uptight and had certain expectations that I built up for how the business and the team and technology should function. All first, second, third, fourth, and fifth attempts to delegate work went poorly. I could not let go of the stories I had about why somebody was not ready for the delegation and why I still needed to be involved. I focused on any aspect of the employee that fit my reasoning of why they would not be successful. The more I focused on those, the more my relationship with the employee degraded, and the more their work degraded too. Over time, I gave up from frustration and amazingly improvements started happening. The less I stressed, the less I focused on what I did not want, the more they started delivering the way I did want. It was not for a couple of years that this all made more sense to me. At the time, I was just happy to be making progress, and they were working finally.

I since learned I can speed up this process by focusing on aspects of the person or their work that does feel good. It always feels better to tell these empowered stories over the powerless and disempowering ones. Feeling better is good for you; it is all for you. It is all about you releasing your resistance. The focus on Bob not delivering is you creating another way for you to keep yourself out of the current of your power. This is likely the place you feel comfortable from the orbits you have created for this experience already.

This is the same issue with the concept and resistance to the notion of working from home. All the resistance to it is there, based on previous thoughts and experiences. They are not the non-resisted current version that is flowing to you. The story about them that you continue to tell yourself creates this resistance; it is this resistance to the improvement. You can just as easily tell a good story about how working from home is advantageous to everyone or you can use the concept of working from home as another thing that keeps you from your current and your power.

It is up to you – right now. It is up to you, always, right now. How do you feel? Do you feel good or bad, and how do you want to feel? What do you want to feel? It is all up to you. Your emotions are always your energetic indicator of energy flow and focus. You do not need to feel lousy about something if you do not want to. You do not need to put your focus toward things that make you feel lousy unless you want to – it's your choice.

You change the television or radio station when you do not like the broadcast; well, you have the same power with your thoughts. Change the broadcast or just stop the broadcast and feel for a while. Your feelings are always an indicator of your energy flow, but sometimes you can't feel them because you are too busy thinking or just have never felt what it's like to allow your vibration to rise when you give up the resistance to it. The next chapter will be all about how you can do that more and more often.

10

TOOLS AND TECHNIQUES FOR CONSISTENT IMPROVEMENT

"Everyone is born a genius, but the process of living de-geniuses them."

— R. BUCKMINSTER FULLER

As with the previous chapters, I'll start with a brief review to make sure you are translating a similar frequency. You started this with the understanding that the universe is in motion, along with you in it. Newton gave humanity's initial understanding of this motion with three laws. They described inertia, force, momentum, and how there is not just a single force. I then took this understanding of movement and extended the concept so all aspects of the universe were moving relative to everything else. This was the basis of Einstein's theory of relativity, which explained how this movement by everything creates the notion of something observing the movement and something to be observed moving. The relationship between these points of perception created relative experiences and perceptions based on the speed of the movements. I then discussed what awareness is, and I shared my understanding that awareness is at the movement level itself.

Movement is self-aware of its movement or vibrational frequency compared to those frequencies around it. You consciously make choices based on these collective understandings, awareness, as it aggregates in the present. Most importantly, you learned that this conscious awareness is a nonphysical aspect of yourself. You learned this from the clear definition of matter, which explicitly states energy, mind, and spirit are separate from all things that are physical in this universe. After this, you then learned how your nonphysical and physical aspects are reflections within different environments, but the laws that you understand from one apply to the laws of the other environments. The behavior changes because the basis of the environment is different, but the concepts of the laws remain consistent and are reflections of each other. Then you learned how this energy flow between your non-physical and physical aspects indicates the future energy flow into your now. You also learned that your emotions are indicators of flow and that the point of blending between your two aspects is called your point of attraction. You blend the conscious energies in this and every moment and can tell how this flow of energy influences you based on how you feel.

Through all this, you learned that your project and employees slow down from resistance. I mentioned it many times and many ways, but this is always the basis. You learned that, as you apply pressure to move the projects faster, you create a greater drag on this person or project by the nature of physically speeding things up. You then learned that this same resistance can be decreased through appreciation of the non-physical movement – the vibration – which increases the frequency of the energy you translate. Non-physically, you don't have resistance, so as you increase appreciation, you don't have a similar construct that slows the movement down; it's nonresistant and always builds. Your appreciation eases the tensions and increases the frequency of your flow of energy. Which increases the power of the current you allow in your now.

All this has come down to understanding that you are two aspects represented by the formula $C^2*M=E=M*C^2$. You understand that a change to one side causes a change to the other side, and you understand that the left side is the non-physical representation and the right side the physical. Both are equal to energy. You can allow it now or you can allow it later. It is always collecting and increasing as you live your life. You will allow the flow it into your now when you are nonresistant and receptive to it.

THOUGHT MOMENTUM

What are some techniques that can be used to improve this flow of energy and your awareness of it?

You need to make sure you remember that all movement is subject to momentum and this momentum can be advantageous to you and detrimental if on the wrong side of it. Your momentum of thought seems to begin when you wake in the morning or from any sleep period. It seems that the momentum of your thought stops when you sleep, and you have a few amazing seconds as you wake that you can control the thoughts from where you left them and the momentum and direction you want to take it now.

Think about how your mind and thoughts work when you are angry with something or somebody. It's nearly impossible to stop thinking about it, and every thought you have on the subject just enrages you more because the momentum keeps increasing. Remember, you have two aspects – a non-resistant, non-physical aspect and a physical, resistant aspect.

Which side do you think is experiencing this anger momentum? Well, if you go back to the previous chapter and review the emotional indicators and what they represent, you know that the emotion of anger is on the lower end. This means that the physical aspect of you in that moment is cutting off the flow of energy into this now. This cutting off is caused by the mental resistance to this new flow of energy. Of course, the positive flow of energy from the nonphysical is blocked in the present by the focus on the injustice that brought about the anger.

You would find that this anger eases if you can take a nap. When you wake from the nap, you have a few precious moments to think something besides the situation that created the anger. If you think about that situation again, you will find that you are still just as angry as before the nap because the non-physical vibration and energy gap is exactly as it was left when sleep started. The challenging but amazing thing you can learn to do is to find new awareness and new points of focus as you wake from this sleep state. If you can find something that feels good, like just thinking about how wonderful and comfortable you feel in this just-waking state or appreciation for this state of being for the sleep you just experienced, focus on that. You will find that you have the control to avoid thinking about the stuff that angers you for longer and longer as you change the momentum to something else. It is this amazing gift as you wake from a sleep state that allows you to make these shifts when you can't otherwise control your momentum of thought.

MEDITATION

Another way to stop this momentum besides sleep is a state of meditation. Meditation means a lot of things to a lot of people. This is my definition of it: meditation is the state of a quieted mind, and in this state of a quiet mind, all resistance stops and your vibration naturally rises. This is what I practice daily.

Concentrating on various aspects of the body or on how love flows from you into the world, which are common images in guided meditations, aren't the same thing as an intentionally-quieted mind. Each of those thoughts could potentially have resistance in them as you think about them in the session. Each of those guided aspects potentially has a thought or movement in your nonphysical vibration that you are resistant too. The point of meditation is to achieve a state of non-resistance for a few moments. It's in this state of non-resistance that you begin to realize and feel the subtle nature of the energy flow and emotional indicators that are so critical to deliberately creating and allowing the experiences you want in this life. It is through chronic practice that resistance is removed from your experience a little more each day. Meditation is completely individualized and something you need to figure out for yourself; nobody can quiet your mind for you. Nobody can feel for you, nobody can vibrate for you, nobody can attract for you. Meditation is the tool through which you can understand your vibration, feelings, and point of attraction.

I do not picture anything when I meditate. When I close my eyes, I see trillions of tiny colorful dots dancing in the darkness. If I picture anything during meditation, it is a relaxed focus on various patterns in the endless dot pattern. I also may count breaths or just listen to my breath thinking "in" and "out" as I start. When my mind drifts to various other thoughts, I gently return my focus to the breath. Depending on how active my mind is, I might spend ninety-nine percent of a fifteen-minute session trying to quiet my mind. I might not be successful at all. You will need to figure out what is right for you. Meditation is the easiest practice possible with the most significant return on invested time and improvement of life overall but does take a little practice to find what is right for you.

How do you know when meditating that you have quieted your mind? What is this mystical sensation and state I've described? I like to describe the sensation as detached from your body, a feeling of warmth and extreme comfort, an inability to distinguish any aspect of your body from another. You may feel a swirling energy guiding your body into movement. It is typical at first that, when you feel this, you will focus on the feeling and lose the sensation. This is just fine. When I first started, I might only reach this quieted state of mind for ten to thirty seconds in a fifteen-minute session. As you grow more accustomed to meditation as a practice, this state is generally easier to attain for longer periods of time. The secret is not to bring focus to your detached, quieted mind but just allow it to be and enjoy the incredible sensations as they flow through your body.

I talked about resistance in every chapter, and you should now understand that it's resistance to change in awareness that leads to problems with people and projects. Creating a consistent meditation practice is the most direct way of more consistent alignment with your two aspects. This alignment means less chronic resistance, which means you will chronically be more up to speed with the current of your projects and people.

If you take the concept of momentum and the notion that sleep pauses your momentum of thought briefly, you understand that you can leverage this concept and change the flow of your day if you can create positive momentum early. I recommend meditating for fifteen to twenty minutes first thing in the morning after you wake, use the restroom, etcetera. Everyday. It is important to start the meditation before you start too much momentum of thought and allow the momentum to get out ahead of you. You want to use the meditation as a way of tuning yourself to the nonresistant and higher frequency of vibrational energy and consciousness that constantly flows to you. This is the purpose of a meditation practice.

Do not start a meditation looking for answers to questions or for solutions to problems. The point is to release resistance. The answer to questions and the solutions to problems naturally occurs as the resistance to the flow of energy is decreased, but do not seek them, for doing so introduces resistance to the meditation. The higher vibrational state you achieve from the meditation and by releasing resistance allows you to translate from the higher frequency of energy. This translation will lead to occurrences in your now that are the answers to the questions and solutions to the problems you want. They will occur to you naturally because you released resistance and received the new energy. Meditation is about quieting your mind and allowing your vibration to rise and return to a non-resistant state – that is it. Do not make it more than that. It is one of my favorite experiences and I look forward to it. I love the feeling of wellbeing that surrounds me when I allow non-resistance in meditation. It's the best feeling.

The added benefit of meditation is that it increases your sensitivity to your emotional indicators and the flow of energy going through you. After a couple of weeks of consistent meditation, you will start to notice that you can tell when your thoughts lead to different energy flow as you feel the energy tighten and tense in your body. This is emotional guidance and is a way of keeping you in less resistant states and keeping you in your current – in your power. It is awesome, it is consistent, and it is always, always, *always* happening.

How do I meditate? I do not make a big deal out of it. I sit in a chair either with my feet on the ground or in a cross-legged or lotus position. I wear comfortable clothes, and I listen to a faint sound that is consistent either from an app, a sound machine, or a fan in the room. I focus on this sound, and as my thoughts drift away from the sound, I simply bring my awareness back to it by finding the faint sound and saying to myself, "I can hear it," and saying it repeatedly. Eventually, because I have no resistance to this sound or to finding it, the focus to find this sound keeps me from thinking any other thoughts, my resistance to the current eases, and my vibration rises. It might be for a few seconds, but it's consistent, and finding that state of nonresistance is so valuable to improving the quality of life, and of course, in context of this book, the speed and success of the projects and people in your life.

APPRECIATION

When I finish meditating, I always write a page or so in a journal about how I want to feel generally during that day. I write about the emotions I love feeling, and I do it in a general way, so I don't create any resistance to the momentum of these emotions and feelings in my life. I am effectively tuning myself, calibrating myself early in the day for the life I want to live and the feelings I want to experience in the day, building my momentum from this place early. It is an amazing process, so simple and easy. I typically write ten to sixteen emotions that I want to feel on top of a page and then write generally how I love feeling those feelings, how I love being in that state, and how I love expressing the feelings.

This is an example:

"Clarity Worthy Abundant Prosperous
Joy Fun Love Kindness
Brilliant Guided Intuitive Eager
Ease Invincible Compassionate Funny.
I love this life experience. I love my time and space reality. I appreciate this experience of being physical and nonphysical, and I love the blend of myself at this moment. I appreciate my clarity. I love feeling clarity of mind and clarity of energy, I love being worthy, I so love how worthy I feel. I love my abundance and prosperity. I especially love the clarity and worthiness I feel for the abundant prosperity flowing into my life. I appreciate feeling clarity. I appreciate feeling my worthiness with clarity. I appreciate when I do not feel clarity for the clarity, I know I will feel later. I love feeling joy. I love being joyful. I love seeing others feel joy. I love bringing others joy. I love expressing joyfully as often as I can. I love fun. I love having fun. I so appreciate the concept of fun. I enjoy seeing others have fun. I appreciate all the fun I have had in my life and all the fun I will have today. I love having fun with others. I love when I can be the conduit through which another's fun flows. I love having fun and flowing an energy of fun freely.
I love, love. I so love, love. I love loving. I love being loved, but I love loving. I love the non-resisting love in the moment. I appreciate feeling love as fully as I do. I appreciate all the time I did not feel love for the experience I now know to be the non-resisted feeling of it.
I love kindness. I so appreciate the kindness in my universe. I love experiencing kindness. I love expressing kindness. I appreciate feeling kind. I love watching others being kind.
I love my brilliance. I so love the brilliance I feel at this moment. I love knowing that my brilliance is related to my frequency and I can align to the frequency of non-resistant infinite intelligence whenever I want. I love my brilliance. I love knowing that brilliance is a measure of how much light is flowing and light flows brighter without resistance. I appreciate my brilliance.
I love being guided. I so love the sense of being guided through this life. I love my intuition and my guidance. I love feeling certain and co-

creating with my guidance. I appreciate how my intuition increases all the time. I appreciate the connection and resonance I feel between my two aspects as the feeling of guidance flows through me.

I love feeling eager. I appreciate the eagerness I feel when I am guided along my path, non-resistant. I so love my intuitive-guided brilliance. I love ease. I love the feeling of ease. I love my life being full of ease. I love ease. I appreciate ease. I appreciate relationships that are easy. I appreciate the flow of ease in all aspects of my life. I appreciate feeling in invincible in my alignment with self. I love feeling non-resistance and invincible. I love feeling the energy of certainty and worthiness coursing through me so strongly. I love feeling the thrill bumps of my alignment. I so appreciate compassion. I love being compassionate. I love sharing and radiating my love compassionately to all who cross my path. I love being funny and feeling funny and experiencing humor. I love this life and all the experience I am having and have had. I love this experience. I love being. I love being me. I love this day."

This is just an example, but as you can tell, it is positive and general. I find it hard to go through a day after starting it with meditation and writing my appreciation for my life that is not full of this momentum of love, light, and clarity. It is so easy and so powerful. It can be done for anything. It takes twenty to twenty-five minutes and changes the life experience with chronic practice.

You could write a similar page or two for any person or project that is currently causing issues in your life. The writing doesn't improve the situations; it doesn't create the improvement, but it does make you less resistant to this flow of energy and the improvement you already created that flows to you in your current constantly, waiting for you to allow it into your now. Write about those people and projects in generally believable and positive ways. This creates the state of being less resistant to the changes in you, and this state of less resistance is what allows the new energy to flow into you and your experience. It is so simple and so powerful. Try it.

WORTHINESS

I think a lot of the challenges people face are created because people don't feel worthy of their greatness. Dare I say that most feel this way? I think most people feel a need to be saved or to do something to feel worthy. What I've described in this book so far has never once stated that you need to do something to feel worthy of this energy flow or even that there is something you can do to stop or start it flowing to you. There is nothing you can do to alter the constant flow of pure, positive energy coming to you at this moment, and this moment, and this moment – all moments. It is coming to you in all moments, and it's your choice to allow it or not. I think there is something powerful about the formula I shared because of these two states of being – worthy or not – and another simple way to see our current focus.

Let's look at the formula again – $C^2*M=E=M*C^2$. You have two aspects – a physical and a nonphysical. The nonphysical side of the equations is $C^2*M=E$ and the physical is $E=M*C^2$. If you remove the math characters, you end up with EMC2 physically and C2ME nonphysical. In this physical world, since you must do something to see yourself -- you must bend, capture, or reflect light so you can see yourself -- I held this equation up to a mirror and got 2CME. The two aspects of the formula state, nonphysical: C2ME, and physical (reflected): 2CME.

I think the profound beauty in this shortened phase is the description of how you see yourself in this world. Are you worthy or do you need salvation?

The non-physical aspect tells us that it is navigational –

just C2 ME. See to me. Just look this way – you are worthy of what you want just to see to yourself and look this way.

The physical aspect reads that you need to do something to be worthy – 2C ME. To see me, you need to do something. You need to make an appointment, you need to be worthy, or you need to be saved.

This can help you when you come to a situation that has you off-balance. You can think if you are seeing it as you are worthy or seeing it as you need to be saved. It is a significant difference in the amount of resistance you would feel, and remember, resistance is everything when feeling good or not.

PLANNING

You have this notion of how the flow of energy works knowing that you can also understand how proper planning and preplanning for things can improve the flow. With projects, you know that good plans are super important, and you pay penalties every time you deviate from the plan. You can also plan how you want your conscious energy to come into your experience, how you resist or not, and how you experience the next moment. Understanding that momentum continues to build until you sleep or meditate matters. You can utilize this positive momentum to increase the speed of projects and people just by removing the resistance as you describe how you think they are performing and whenever you describe or think about how they are performing. Each time you describe it as working well or almost failing, you create this path in your future collection of energy and expectations of momentum. In fact, most of the success you have influencing projects and people comes from the thoughts and narratives you tell yourself about those relationships when they are not actively present. All those thoughts are preparing the course and path for that rendezvous and the relationship you have with it well before you have the experience.

There are so many ways to release resistance, and I have just shared a couple. Remember, it is so useful to start your day and build your momentum of success, joy, and happiness early. It is so useful and powerful in your life to get out ahead of the challenges. The improvements are done now in your asking; you just need to find a way to realize it, receive it, allow it, and actualize it into your experience. It is a truly beautiful experience, and I'm so excited for you.

OBSTACLES AND BUMPS ALONG THE WAY

"The snake which cannot cast its skin has to die. As well the minds which are prevented from changing their opinions; they cease to be mind."

— FRIEDRICH NIETZSCHE

At this point, you've come so far and have the potential of an empowered perspective of yourself and how you influence the projects and people in your life. It's my hope that, at this stage, you are starting to see the concepts and matters in your life as aspects of resistance to movement. You understand now that you have a relationship with these concepts and matters and that your perspective of this relationship with them is your focus. In turn, this focus creates the opportunity to increase wherever it is placed. You've learned that this increase is caused by our awareness, and the longer you focus on anything, the greater the awareness of that thing becomes. You learned that this awareness is a non-physical aspect of our being. You then learned the different behaviors of some universal laws depend on whether they were operating on the physical or the non-physical and how this reflectivity creates a flow of energy between both aspects. Then you learned that this flow of energy is indicated by your emotions and that it is an up-to-the-moment indicator. It is real-time. It is indicating based on what you think about right now. You learned that all these concepts work non-physically with the concept of momentum and that non-physical movement doesn't have friction to slow the momentum down. Everything is additive – everything. Then you learned some techniques to help you leverage and control more of your momentum that always adds to your experience.

The aspects of your projects and people situations, as you see them right now, are based on your relationships with the various concepts and characters involved in the narrative that you tell yourself about each of them. You learned also the physical world seeks empirical evidence based on the result of force, or the result of movement. This force leads you to try to motivate your teams to make the projects go faster; they must take more action. You apply more pressure and ask for more output from the team. You develop stories about their success and failure. You come to a "plan B" because you lose faith in the team and think you need to change the delivery.

In the new work-from-home world, you create resistance to success by holding onto the concepts of how things worked in an office scenario and not allowing the new way of working from a home environment to be and grow; this is resistance. The story you tell about how you need to be in an office, how you need to be close to make these choices, how it's more convenient, how workflow was, how you got more done, etcetera, are all the stories you tell that are indicators of your resistance for the current flow.

This process is so simple. The formula is as simple a

description of the universal experience as any I've ever seen. It describes the co-creative nature of all things along with the eternal evolution. $C\char`\^2*M=E=M*C\char`\^2$ is an evolved way of understanding your place in this world and how you create the experience you have.

The single most important take-away from this book is that resistance both slows stability and creates stability. There are times for both. It depends on the need you have now which you should focus upon. Do you want people to move faster and get more done? Focus on the stability they have from the current resistance as a platform to bounce off and create more, embrace the resistance, and appreciate it for all that it brings you. Remember, this appreciation always increases the frequency of the energy you are able to translate in the present, and in doing this, you will start to have new perceptions and new thoughts that lead you to the ideas and conversations that will always increase the project deliverables.

My dream for anybody reading this book is to understand how important resistance is to your experience in this life and how you can utilize it and leverage it in the best way possible. I dream you will understand more about how incredibly unique and special you are as a point of focus in this universe and how incredibly powerful your point of focus is for building the life you desire. I want your projects to be wild successes. I want your teams to perform better than they have ever performed before. Most importantly, I want you to feel more joy and love in this life, regardless of where you focus.

LOVE

Another way to see this energy flow is one of love. In every moment, you have the choice of flowing this energy – this love – or you have the choice to restrict it. It is your only real choice. All other choices grow from this understanding. Your only choice in every moment is how much love you choose to flow or resist, and more importantly, whose love is it that you are resisting? It is self-love; it is the love and improvement you created for yourself by living your life and learning what you didn't want so the non-resistant side could expand and include what you did want. My dream for you is that you will find and allow this flow more and more. The words of this book and the perspectives shared will make more sense to you as you go forward and have more experiences. These words may sneak back into your mind to remind you at the perfect time that it is your perception that matters in this world for you. Are you perceiving your worthiness or your need to overcome something to feel worthy?

The concepts in this book are simple but incredibly deep. As you start to create a more deliberate experience by bringing more and more awareness of your emotions and to your energy flow, there are some obstacles that get in the way of success.

OBSTACLES

All the obstacles are effectively resistance to the improvement you want to create. It is not different from this process as it is with the projects and people you are trying to influence. Through meditation, you will begin to understand where your emotional set point is. That is the emotional energy flow you default back to when not being deliberate. This set point is the default place you create from, meaning that if you have knee-jerk reactions to most conversations about how stupid people are and how they are trying to ruin you, that story tells you that your emotional set point is one that is quite cut off from the energy flow and focused on blame. It is low in the emotional guidance scale. Does that make sense?

When you get more in touch with your emotions and can start to feel the subtle changes and shifts of them and your energy flow, as you have different points of focus in the day, you can start to mold the thought paths more and more. Until that time, you need to pay attention to the stories that you tell or to the narratives of your thoughts and conversations with others. These narratives provide the indicator for where that energy flow is; you just need to listen to them.

For example, if you are constantly telling a story of how a coworker is brilliant but so lazy, you are splitting the energy related to that person. There is not a positive momentum that is possible because there is a little good and a little bad. Quite frankly, it is my observation that this is how almost all people speak until they understand this deliberate path more. Most people will always give a little good and a little bad. Do you know what this causes, given all this new knowledge up to now? It causes uncertainty, and it leads to momentum being built toward both what is wanted (the brilliant teammate) and unwanted (the lazy teammate). There isn't one that outweighs the other, so this story is one of disempowerment and confusion. You learned that you could change this narrative to only "the coworker is brilliant," and leave it there. This starts a positive momentum. After all, it's your relationship with what you consider hard work and productivity that says this person isn't working hard and is lazy. It's your relationship with this person, and remember, this relationship defines your experience. In Chapter 5, you learned how all life and awareness is about the observation and relationship of that observation; it's exactly like that when you observe another on your team too.

You have the control to create your life the way you want it to be. You have control to create the projects and teams the way you envision them being, and you also have the control to keep those creations from ever becoming part of your experience. It's my dream for you that, by the end of this book, you will understand this simple concept and start to bring more awareness to your flow of energy and your emotional narratives more, and more, and more.

What I've found is that any narrative you have been telling for a while (most often) is laden with resistance to what you want. It is just full of words and concepts that are no longer serving you, yet you find it necessary to retell the story. In fact, it is often like you are trying to justify that you want to do better by explaining why you have not done it yet. This, again, is my dream for you – realizing that it is not about where you have been but about where you want to go.

What does it cost you if you don't change or adjust your perspective? Well, nothing really. You will not feel as joyful or as happy as you could otherwise, and you will continue to think of the world as a struggle instead of as a co-creating partner that wants the best for you. You will put forth more and more energy to make the projects move faster and to make people get more things done. This is the energy of motivation or forcing mass to accelerate through physical means. This entire book is about the power of your inspiration and how to inspire yourself and your team. It is not by trying hard to find inspiration. It is by relaxing and allowing it because it is who you are when you don't resist it. The entire concept of this book is about relaxing and allowing the amazing life you have been creating to flow more into your now experience more so than you've allowed ever before.

There is one more thing I want to share: simply the joy of the flow. As you allow this more and grow more in tune with your nonphysical self and the guidance always coming your way, you'll start to feel how the universe is trying, at every moment, to knock your socks off with the delivery of all you want. It is constant; I cannot stress this enough. The flow to you is constant, but the ability to realize and actualize it is yours and yours alone. It is my dream for you to feel this flow more and more. It is the most fun and satisfying way to experience life I've yet found – delightful.

The concepts shared in this book have been generically related to projects and people. The concepts can, and do, obviously apply to life much more broadly, and I'm sure I'll write a few books on other topics that bridge the gaps there too.

You are the creator of your creation. You are the flow and restriction of the energy of your life. You created it, you modified it, and you allowed it. All of it is created by you, for you, and is flowing to you and through you constantly. This book will help bring more awareness to this flow, and if you remember from a previous chapter, a mind once stretched to a new idea can never return to its original dimension. There is no going back with the knowledge you now have; there is only going forward and allowing it to become so much more within you and within all those you are interested in.

I want you to feel better. I want your projects to succeed. I want you to feel more ease and relief interacting with your teams. I want you to understand it's about allowing, not resisting. It's about appreciating, not forcing. I want you to find appreciation for the process of the projects and personal interactions. The process and its details are so important. Mostly, it's about the relationship you have with yourself. It is there. It is eternal and it is guiding you to all that you want and have already created. This relationship with yourself is the foundation to all other relationships. Cultivate your awareness of it more often with more appreciation, and you will cultivate improvements to all aspects of your project and team relationships as well.

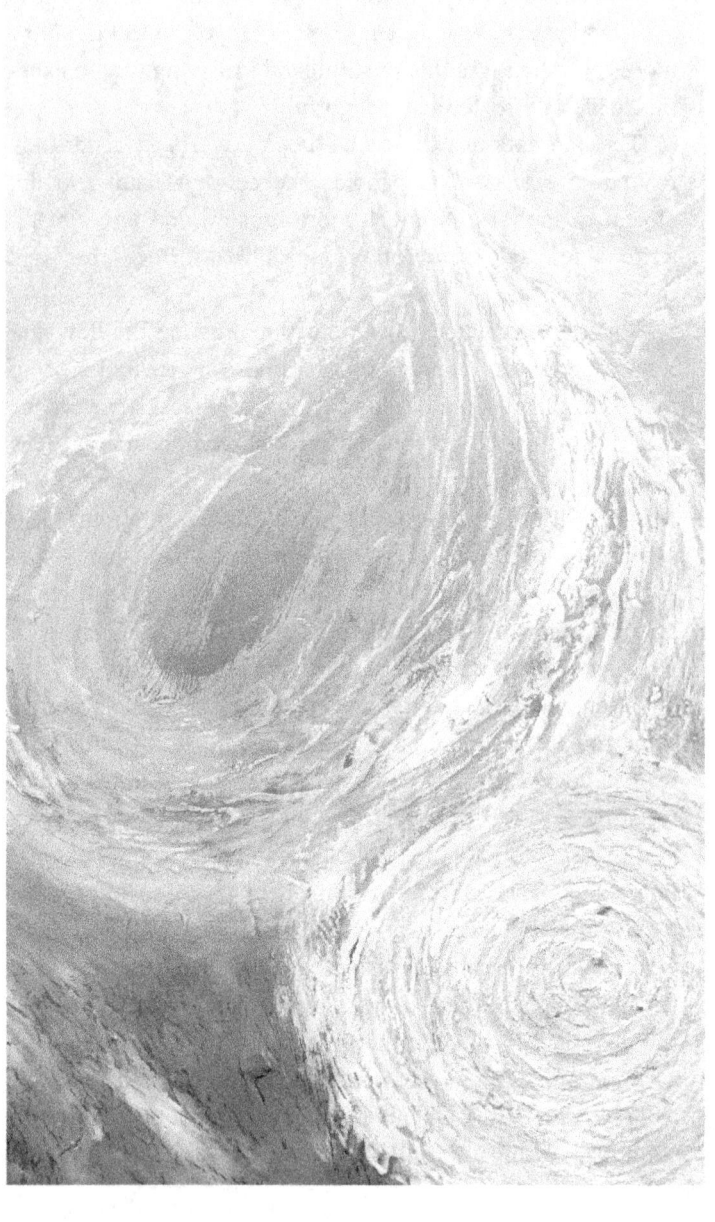

12

RELIEF FROM PROJECT STRESS, BELIEF IN PROJECT SUCCESS

"Always be yourself, express yourself, have faith in yourself, do not go out and look for a successful personality and duplicate it."

— BRUCE LEE

By this point, I hope you feel how the improvement for your projects is within you, that you realize how much of your relationship with the movement of the projects matters, and you realize how the history of perceptions you have about your teammates can be limiting and empowering.

It is awesome to be here and have more knowledge and understanding of how you create your experience in this universe. It is awesome to understand that you can influence it or allow it to unfold by default.

It is incredible to be here and now and understand how your flow of energy is indicated to you constantly throughout living your life. It's so amazing to know that you can tell from your emotions at this moment how much of the energy of desire you have built up and collected through living life.

In each moment, it is fantastic to know that you can flow love or restrict it. It is empowering to know that you only have this choice and the rest is molded around it.

It is awesome to know that when things are tense, you can increase the frequency of the thought that was tense by appreciating aspects of it. It is awesome to know that, as you increase that frequency of energy for that translation of thought, you will get to less tension and will get to higher-powered, more powerful thoughts.

It's advantageous to know that momentum of thought is controllable and can be leveraged. It's necessary to know that momentum works with thought just like it does with physical objects.

The coolest part about being here in this book is realizing how specifically amazing the universe is just for you and how you are central to your experience. How amazing is that? It should be the most amazing thing to you, for this whole universe is your playground. It doesn't need to be the challenge and struggle you make it out to be; it's supposed to be fun. Did you follow the flow of energy? You create the refined improvement in your future, and you get to control when, and if, you allow that energy into your experience. How is it not supposed to be fun when you realize this concept? It's about you being the central aspect of yourself.

The projects you have are aspects of you, and the people on your projects are another aspect of you. Do you feel worthy of their success – truly? Do you feel worthy of your greatness? Do you feel worthy of your team's greatness? Do you feel worthy when I tell you that you are central to your universal experience or do you say, "bullcrap?" Remember, the choice in the perspective is all yours to have, and both perspectives are accurate for you. One will feel better, and one will feel worse. One will feel empowering, one will feel disempowering – it's up to you.

You now know there is a current of energy running to you continually in the present moment. This is the gift your awareness gave to you for all time, and it is the ability to define those experiences that you want to have, the things you want to feel, and allow or deny them.

A friend, Tony, and I had talked through their business idea several times over an eighteen-month period. At the start, Tony had poor clarity about what he wanted to do, but felt deeply he wanted to help the world because of all the pain in it and dire problems that appear to be increasing in scale and magnitude. During the first conversation, he was emotional and obviously cared immensely about the state of the world. Tears came to his eyes as he talked through the suffering he observed when he traveled the globe a few years earlier. I wanted to help him. I wanted to help this world he described, it sounded so opposite the world I am describing in this book.

During the first conversation, I talked through my understanding of the laws of the universe and how his focus matters. I compassionately saw his pain, and, through as much kindness as I could provide at the time, I began to explain that his focus and conclusions were just and logical. That there were terrible atrocities in the world, and he could find them everywhere he wanted to look. He could also find the beauty in these same experiences if he understands this flow of energy and his evolving awareness of it. In a rudimentary way, I further stated that his focus on these peoples' pain and suffering took him away from his power, from his current. His focus on their lack and their struggle caused him to resist and block his flow. This is not because they weren't suffering and experiencing horrible amounts of lack. It is because it invalidates his inner knowing about the growing expansion of awareness and energy flow in the universe and how they, too, have access to this source of power, their source of power. Further, the focus on their pain creates more of it in his awareness as he expands forward, which means the more he looks at their suffering, the more reasons for their suffering he sees. Further, when he looked at these groups suffering, I explained he felt the pain of the group which is far greater than the pain of a single individual within the group. That is an enormous amount of energy to take on for himself and should be profoundly overwhelming.

Why is this wrong? It's not. It is just that it is disempowering for you if it feels lousy when you focus upon it. That is it. Disempowering means you are not powering your reality with as much current as you could. You are taking power away from yourself. In taking power away, you slow down. The more power you take away, the more you slow down. At some point, it feels like the world is speeding up, which it is. Time in this high-resistance perspective is speeding up because you have slowed so much.

Tony left this meeting telling me I was an idiot and naïve in the ways of the world. It was not ideal or my desired way to have it end, but I honored his opinion. Really, before I understood the system I described in this book, I would agree with him too. The best I could do, right then, was honor and validate his perspective. It was not my place to do anything further. They were his expansions of mind and conscious energy that he had to realize and actualize. I would never want to steal that experience from him or anybody. It's the best feeling he could have, and one that I knew he would have eventually, and the path to that was not for me to define it was for him to unwrap.

A few months passed, and Tony reached back out to me. This time he was sad, like really, really sad. I could tell immediately from his voice something was wrong. He said he continued to focus on the suffering of the world and grew angrier and angrier with it. He felt such a profound need to help and to be of service to his fellow human that he was dying inside because he wasn't doing enough about it.

I drove over to Tony's house, and we talked for a while before I started in on my philosophical perspective. Eventually I explained the following to him: the sadness isn't coming from his focus on the suffering as much as it's coming from the resistance of energy into his life. If he could compassionately look at the suffering with sympathy and not empathy, he would be able maintain his positive energy flow. His description of dying inside was spot on. I further explained how he was literally cutting off his life force energy with his continued focus on the suffering and the resulting vibrational disharmony it produced in him. It wasn't the suffering, at this point, that was his problem, it was all the expansion he created in his physical asking and nonphysical answering when he focused on the suffering. This expansion in his conscious energy was raging to come into his experience and his continued focus toward what wasn't wanted to keep it from being realized by him and actualized through him. After a couple of hours of talking, I left Tony and recommended a solid practice of meditation combined with not focusing on others suffering for a while. I further explained he needed to solve his energetic gaps before he could find the solutions he had created already for others.

A couple of months later, Tony reached back out. He sounded so much better on the phone this time. He was energetic and sounded empowered. He explained that he did make a daily meditation practice a priority after our last conversation. He praised how it took the edge of his emotional turmoil and how he loved the sense of well-being he felt meditating. Tony described a positive outlook on his life. It was refreshing and so much more pleasant to be around.

Further, Tony told me he was having the most amazing

ideas on how to help the people less fortunate than him and how these ideas just lit him up with excitement. At this point, he started to tell a story about his disempowerment again about how he didn't think he would ever take one of these ideas and do anything with it. I asked him to stop his self-restricting narration. I explained that the thoughts he was having were the energy gap between his two aspects closing. He was receiving and allowing the new energy, and that each time he did, it felt amazing to feel this realization of the energy flow.

I recommended that he just appreciate each one for the experience of the flow. Not to feel compelled to get started and deliver the idea, but to embrace that he was finding nonresistance and receiving the improved vibrational translations of this new conscious energy. I explained how ideas must go through a process of gestation before they are born into the manifestation. This gestation period was for him to enjoy as he built the momentum of his concepts to the point they actualized with ease; with ease because he was up to speed with the energy and everything was the next logical step. I also shared there would not be a struggle, it would not be hard, and when the time was right for the idea to be born into the objective world, it would flow for him in a series of logical next steps and occurrences.

A few months later, Tony called me again. This time he was just elated with life. It wasn't in the same place, so it was a bit hard for me at first, I was a bit down for some reason that day. For the first time, I can remember his energy trained mine up during the conversation, and I was able to meet him on his high-flying flow. He told me that he did what I suggested, and much to his delight, his ideas continued to grow and gestate. He explained how the feeling of this new energy flow was an amazing leverage in all his work. He was using the power of his momentum of thought and positive energy to start a new business that was going to help build and fund schools in a number of poor countries. He explained how, in the past six weeks, he randomly met all the right people to bring it together. He described the experience as magic, as a miracle for where he once was to what he was now creating.

I was so happy for him, truly. Even as I write this now and think about to the moment of this call, my eyes fill with tears of love and joy. I was not filled with joy because he was helping impoverished people, I was filled with joy because he understood the power and flow of love in this universe. He made it past blame and disempowerment to his find his empowerment which allowed his realization of the solution and the perfectly actualized timing of the rendezvous with the right people helping make Tony's vision objectified and real. Tony found the way to receive and allow more love through him, and in doing so, improve the objective reality for all. This book is my flow of love to you.

THE UPLIFTING CLOSE

You now know how to create a better feeling narrative to the story. Even if right here and now, you feel you aren't quite there, you can still create a better narrative with something like the following I wrote. You can, of course, use this or, better yet, create your own. It is more empowering for you to create your own, but this is a good example of an uplifting, nonresistant narration.

"I know I am a deliberate creator. I know I don't always create deliberately right now; I know that most often I don't deliberately create at all, but I have had the experience and I know I can do it. I know that each time I deliberately change my thought from something that doesn't feel good to something that feels better, I am

strengthening the positive narrative in my life for that thought, and this builds momentum. I so love the fairness of momentum. I love that momentum doesn't care if it's a good energy flow or one that doesn't feel so good, and the continual focus on it will increase the momentum of that.

I love that consistency of the universe, and I will use it more and more to my advantage. I love knowing that my perspective of a project is relative to me and I can control my perspective by being aware of how my thoughts feel when I think of them. I so love knowing that I can empower my team through a positive narrative. I love knowing that I don't have to power my team; I don't have to force them to improve, I simply need to release the resistance to the improvement that already exists, and that they are working toward. I love knowing that I can mold my life experience in these ways. I love knowing I can be of most value and service to others when I am powered with my current in my now. I love knowing that the better mood I am in, the more energy I am flowing, and the more energy I am flowing, the more value I bring to those my life touches.

I love knowing that this is supposed to be fun. I love having fun. I love the fun of completing projects on time. I love how the business responds to my complete projects. I love how the team feels so positive as they come together and complete the necessary work. I love how the team finds inspiration in the details of the project to keep their mood and attitude high. I love being a positive influence on this team. I love that they work from home so well now. I love the freedom I am giving my team as they work from home and deliver more than ever before. I love knowing that the location of the team doesn't matter because my perceptions of what is occurring is the way I see the world; it is the lens that I see and experience the world through, and I love knowing that this experience is one that I control and define.

I love being the creator of my creative life experience. I love helping my team and company excel. I love feeling a part of something more. I love being a part of more and creating a culture of worthiness. I so love how I've learned all I have and now know that I am directly responsible for my life experience – not so much the events that occur, for some of those have massive amounts of momentum that I can't change at this point, but I love knowing that my perspective, my mood, and my attitude are controllable.

My vibration is controllable. I love how my vibration is controllable. I love how I now know what nonphysical vibration is and how it influences me in all I do. I love translating thought. I love receiving thought, and I love allowing energy. I also love uplifting my team and company. I love the success we are finding and the success we will continue to find. I love the challenges we have had, for the definition of what we want has come from these challenges. I love knowing that these challenges are the contrast I've created to better define those things that I want. I love knowing that I can feel this energy build up and this energy alignment. I love knowing that this energy alignment can help guide me to all that I want. I love knowing that you understand these concepts more and more. I love knowing that today you have a new perspective and today everything changes."

I want you to feel relief regarding the stress of the projects. I want you to feel relief in the performance of your teammates and employees, and I want this relief, for in it you will ease the tensions of the energy flow within you. In this improved energy, you will find a new perspective, new thoughts, and new occurrences that matter. It is tuning into the solution, not the problem. It is allowing the flow of energy to happen and not resist it. It is an art form. It is so easy once you get the hang of it. You will soon feel all your projects speed up and teammates deliver more than ever. You will feel like you are magical as you get the hang of this, but it's not magic; it's law. It's universal law, so leverage it. You're supposed to; it's here for you.

I started this book with a quote from Eisenhower about leadership. It described how people through their own desire to complete something are more powerful than when they are forced. This applies to our self-leadership as well as whatever you add to the team and project dynamic. Are you in your power? Are you allowing the current that is everything you want to flow in and power your now, or are you resisting and recreating from the resistance that already is?

At this point, after reading the preceding uplifting narration, you should be on a higher frequency with less resistance and be able to bring more to the leadership of yourself and your teams. You understand why it matters now in a way you probably never have before. You understand how you are always in control of your energy and it gets easier the more you bring awareness to it. I so love knowing that the more you practice this, the better and more fluid you become at it, which of course only makes it that much easier to practice. I'm so certain of your success. I'm so excited for you to grow to feel this certainty too.

I've loved this experience. I've loved writing a book explaining how you, as the perceiver, create the awareness of resistance to your projects and team's success chronically from your awareness of the past. Now you find empowerment through the new awareness of your energy flow and its creative potential. I love sharing how you can change your perspective, and I also love sharing how it works and why it works when you do. I hope you find it valuable. I've had so much fun sharing.

Until we speak again, may you feel the constant blend of love and light at this moment as it guides you to everything you desire.

ACKNOWLEDGMENTS

Mom, thank you for my life. I love it. I love you.

Jess, thank you for co-creating the greatest kid ever. I love him; he's a treasure.

Diego, thank you for being. You are the greatest, I'm so proud of you. I adore watching you become you. I love you.

Eva, thank you for the freedom and reflections. Always the perfect place and the perfect time. I love you.

Isaac, thank you for the foundations.

Albert, thank you for relating so well.

Abraham, thank you for the inspiration and co-creation. It's been indescribably fun.

Everybody at The Author Incubator, you didn't just make the book possible, you made it a complete pleasure all along the way.

Thank you.

ABOUT THE AUTHOR

Nicholas Ferguson is a technical advisor who has helped financial companies scale and expand for twenty years through various mentoring, guidance, engineering, and architecture roles.

His life largely characterized by a pioneering spirit – from his early rejection of school systems to the culmination of his life's understanding – he always prefers the path less traveled. Nicholas loves painting, technology, yoga, meditation, and cartoons.

Nicholas spends most days, when not at a keyboard typing away, pondering the meaning of life and creating new paintings that somehow speak a meaning of his last understanding about the universe. It's here where Nicholas is most delighted, surrounded by the people and things he loves most, listening to nature and creating layers and layers of intrinsic meaning to him.

He was gifted with a childhood relatively free of dogmatic beliefs or mandatory practices. Truly, he has led a life toward an intimate understanding of the intelligence, kindness, and compassion of the universe. It's this understanding he loves to share most with any who is willing to listen with an open mind. He believes in the goodness and interconnectedness of all and celebrates the diversity of choice in the universe for the stability it creates.

Born in Colorado, Nicholas is a single father, joyfully living in Franklin, Tennessee, with his son and puppy.

ABOUT DIFFERENCE PRESS

Difference Press is the exclusive publishing arm of The Author Incubator, an educational company for entrepreneurs – including life coaches, healers, consultants, and community leaders – looking for a comprehensive solution to get their books written, published, and promoted. Its founder, Dr. Angela Lauria, has been bringing to life the literary ventures of hundreds of authors-in-transformation since 1994.

A boutique-style self-publishing service for clients of The Author Incubator, Difference Press boasts a fair and easy-to-understand profit structure, low-priced author copies, and author-friendly contract terms. Most importantly, all of our #incubatedauthors maintain ownership of their copyright at all times.

LET'S START A MOVEMENT WITH YOUR MESSAGE

In a market where hundreds of thousands of books are published every year and are never heard from again, The Author Incubator is different. Not only do all Difference

Press books reach Amazon bestseller status, but all of our authors are actively changing lives and making a difference.

Since launching in 2013, we've served over 500 authors who came to us with an idea for a book and were able to write it and get it self-published in less than 6 months. In addition, more than 100 of those books were picked up by traditional publishers and are now available in bookstores. We do this by selecting the highest quality and highest potential applicants for our future programs.

Our program doesn't only teach you how to write a book – our team of coaches, developmental editors, copy editors, art directors, and marketing experts incubate you from having a book idea to being a published, bestselling author, ensuring that the book you create can actually make a difference in the world. Then we give you the training you need to use your book to make the difference in the world, or to create a business out of serving your readers.

ARE YOU READY TO MAKE A DIFFERENCE?

You've seen other people make a difference with a book. Now it's your turn. If you are ready to stop watching and start taking action, go to http://theauthorincubator.com/apply/.

"Yes, I'm ready!"

OTHER BOOKS BY DIFFERENCE PRESS

Love Avatar: Unleash Your Divine Feminine Superpowers and Awaken the Goddess Within by Lord Coltrane

Your Script for Intimacy: Fix Your Marriage and Your Sex Life by Dr. Petra Frese

Life after Child Loss: The Mother's Survival Guide to Cope and Find Joy by Peggy Green

Money Blocks: 8 Steps to Get to Six Figures in 90 Days or Less in Any Economy by Vivian S. De Guzman, RPT, MBA

The New Management Blueprint: Spark Talent to Ignite Winning Teams and Create Valuable Results by Michelle Hoffmann

Six-Figure Health Coach: The 12-Step Blueprint to Doing the Significant, Soul-Satisfying Work You Love by Shaunna Menard, MD

Goodbye Adrenal Fatigue: The Step-By-Step Healing Companion Guide by Carmen Leung

The Ultimate Guide to Support Your Girlfriend with MS: Tools and Techniques to Help Her Manage Multiple Sclerosis by Kathi Million

Plan the Birth You Want without Fear: A Guide to Creating Your Dream Delivery by Maricea Muhammad, RN, MSN, MHA, UZIT

Know Your Angels: Embracing the Angels' Messages and Love into Your Life by Lannie Reid

THANK YOU

Thank you so much for reading this book. I know you are already on a pathway of accelerated success and prosperity from the expansion experienced reading. I also know the concepts expressed in this book are bold and new, so I'd like to offer you as much assistance in understanding them as possible.

If you would like to reach out, please send an email to, nick@njf.io.

I love sharing these concepts; it's the most fun for me. And, I know in a short time you'll experience similar love for your project challenges as you accelerate past them with more ease than ever before. I'm so excited for your success. It's going to feel so wonderful as that project stress eases away and you feel powered by the current more and more.

www.ingramcontent.com/pod-product-compliance
Lightning Source LLC
Chambersburg PA
CBHW052352220526
45465CB00003BA/1075